THE CHRISTIAN ESCAPE FROM T

DEPRESSION

SUE SAXON

Published by New Day Publications 2007

ISBN No. 0-9544244-1-7

ACKNOWLEDGEMENTS

With grateful thanks to Eileen and Harry for their expert help and advice in typing and reading this manuscript, and to Andrew Holland for his cover design.

I am indebted to Hazel, Andrea and Peter, without whose encouragement I might never have finished the task, also to Rebecca who every day helps turn around difficult situations.

Finally to all of those who have been honest enough to share their walk through depression with me, you know who you are and you have helped me more than you could ever know.

FOREWORD

'It felt like walking through treacle...'
'Like a big black hole I couldn't climb out of...'
'Like cotton wool between my ears'

However you wish to describe your view of depression, you have probably picked up this book hoping that you would find the magic wand to wave within its pages. If only there was some 'quick fix' solution which would make all your symptoms disappear overnight.

If you were hoping for the advice that you could be cured by tomorrow (or even tonight, if only you could pray longer or harder or had enough positive thinking) then this is not the book for you.

This book is for those who want to include spiritual solutions as well as real, practical advice, along with helpful understanding of the issues involved for those who are depressed and their loved ones.

Together we will explore some possible courses of action, while you **take** your prescribed medication, or while you wait for your **doctor's** referral, or while you are in between all of that and waiting to **get better**.

At the end of each chapter there are Bible references as well as **clear**, achievable lifestyle **goals**. Make sure you write down each verse in the reference, even if learning the verse seems impossible at this moment in time. As you look at the goals, make sure you attempt each one, before moving on and adding the next goal.

The aim is, that by the time you have reached the end of the book, become more familiar with what God actually says in His Word and made each goal a normal part of your day to day life, you will be feeling much more positive.

Our plan is that, by taking small steps each day, you will, over a period of time, have the hope that you **can get better**, and be able to escape the jungle of depression.

CONTENTS

Throughout the book, wherever resources are denoted by use of *,
further information is included in the List of Helps at the end of the book.

CHAPTER 1 WHAT IS DEPRESSION?

This book is not an attempt to bring a clinical diagnosis for your condition, nor is it a layman's guide to Psychiatry in three easy lessons, but simply a jargon-free attempt to explain how you might be feeling, and what you might do to help you get better.

If this is the first time you have faced this situation, it might have crept up on you over a period of time. If you have been feeling 'down' for four weeks or more, with feelings of hopelessness and despair, as if the future is not worth living, then you are probably clinically depressed.

You should definitely make an appointment to see your GP at the first opportunity. **Do not make the mistake** of thinking that you will sort it out on your own. If you could have done that already, you would not still be feeling as you do and would probably not be reading this book.

You might think because you are a Christian, you should never become depressed, or that it is all your own fault, or even that this has happened because of some unconfessed sin in your life. Spend a few moments in prayer, considering if there is some aspect of your behaviour, habits or relationships that could be wrong. Ask God to reveal anything that is wrong, then confess it and move on in your thoughts.

We will come back to this in a later chapter, but for now it will be less than helpful for you to continue to be preoccupied with what you may (or may not) have done wrong, 'beat yourself up' over your perceived failure and then decide that you are not worthy to ever get well again.

As a Christian, you might only want to look for a 'miraculous' recovery from your depression. In your Church, the leaders might teach that if you are a Christian you should never get sick and that if the unthinkable ever happens to you, the only valid healing is a miraculous overnight one.

The fact is that all true healing is valid. Whether healing for a physical illness happens instantly or even overnight, or if someone has a psychosomatic illness which gradually gets better through prayer and counselling, it is **no less a healing**. If a Christian has a headache and takes something as basic as an aspirin, should he be guilt-ridden or experience regret?

When we read in the Bible (Mark Chapter 8 verse 22) about the blind man being healed at a place called Bethsaida, I do not remember the man receiving the healing being disappointed that it 'took two goes' before he was healed, or even whether he was disappointed that something as basic as spit was involved!

What about the man born blind described in John Chapter 9 verse 1? For his healing, Jesus not only spat on the ground, but also made mud and applied it to his eyes. Then for the final stage of the healing, this man who had only been used to begging before, had to go and wash in the pool at Siloam, before he came home seeing!

It should be noted that everyone around this man had an opinion about his situation. At the beginning, the disciples wanted Jesus to confirm that this man's blindness was due to sin - either his own sin or his parents' sin - but Jesus very clearly stated that sin was not the issue here.

Then, after the healing, his neighbours concluded that this was not the same man who had come back healed – it only looked like the man! For the neighbours, it was easier to 'invent' an identical twin for this man than it was to accept that he was now healed!

For the Pharisees standing by, the main issue was that all this healing had happened on the Sabbath, which was unlawful.

But what about the parents? They could only say 'We **know** he is our son.....We **know** he was born blind....but how he can see now, or who opened his eyes, we don't know.......ASK HIM.' For them the issue was not **how** or even **how long**, but the facts spoke for themselves, they **knew** their son was healed. They directed their focus on the main thing.

So, if you are a Christian who is struggling with depression, do not get caught up with anything other than the main thing. Do not become obsessed about how long you have been depressed, or whether it was caused by sin, or whether your healing and recovery will only be worthwhile if it happens instantly, after some (well known) person has prayed for you.

It might come as a surprise to you to discover that most Christians (myself included) believe that God has given many gifts to His Church and some of them are called doctors. If Jesus could use mud, I don't have a problem believing that God could also use a doctor to help you get better, do you?

Do not put it off even one day longer, put this book down now and make that appointment! Done that? Good – now you have taken control of that, you can carry on reading. People put off that step for all sorts of reasons, but none of them will help you get better, which is what we are working together to achieve.

If, up till now, you have avoided seeing your doctor, your reason may be that you are simply too depressed to get up in the morning to phone the doctor's surgery. Well, try phoning in the afternoon, or checking if there is a mental health team listed in your phone book, where you could phone and arrange for someone to see you.

On the other hand, it may be that you feel ashamed that you are depressed and you think you should be able to 'pull yourself together' or 'get out of it'. You may feel that your doctor is going to judge you as being somehow weak because you are feeling as you do. Can I ask you whether you would consider going to see the doctor if you had a sore throat, or a broken leg?

Most people would try to cure the sore throat for a few days themselves, before consulting a doctor. If they had a broken leg, they would make a hospital visit right away if they wanted to get better. Neither scenario would get better if they waited six weeks, just hoping it would sort itself out.

With problems of depression, you should no more feel ashamed or embarrassed than you would do if you had a broken leg and needed medical treatment. One of the facts about depression is that it will make you feel isolated, as if you are not worthy to take part in life, as if no-one has ever felt the way you do.

The truth is that if you were to conduct a survey of the whole population, around one in three people would say that they have struggled with feelings of depression at one time or another (and the other two out of three people may not be telling the truth!)

You may feel that the doctor will not be caring or understanding, or not know how to help you. The truth is that your GP may have already seen three or four patients today before you arrived, with varying symptoms of depression and has probably put a plan of care into action for each one of them, so why should you be any different?

You may be afraid that because you feel so low, you may not be able to get your words out without crying when you finally get to see your doctor. If that is the fear which prevents you getting to see your GP, then look at the possibility of taking a close friend or family member with you, for emotional support.

Or if you prefer to go alone, write down a few lines on a piece of paper explaining how you are feeling and how long you have been feeling this way and pass this to the doctor as you sit down.

Make sure it is just a few lines though, not a sequel to 'War & Peace'! - your doctor will probably have a surgery full of patients waiting to see him and if you give him a few clues, he will know which questions to ask you, in order to arrive at the correct diagnosis.

Consider writing something like this:
I have been feeling depressed since February.
I have panic attacks if I am left on my own.
I am not sleeping or eating well.
I have stopped meeting up with my friends.
I can't face going to work.

Armed with this information, your doctor should be able to point you in the direction of the help you are likely to need. Do not come out of the surgery disappointed if you have not been given a prescription for medication.

Your doctor may feel that the best course of action for you is some counselling, or talking therapy. Do not think that your doctor is not 'up to the job' if he has referred you to see someone else. He will almost certainly want you to have some routine blood tests - just to ensure that there is no underlying physical reason for your depression, such as under-active thyroid function.

If he has decided that you need to see a specialist at a hospital or mental health team, he has taken that decision based on all the facts available and because he wants you to see the person most likely to have the training and the time available to be able to help you. Just make sure you keep the appointment, when it arrives, even if you have had to wait longer than you would like.

On the other hand, your GP may prescribe some tablets which he thinks could help you. Make sure you take them regularly and he will also probably suggest that you go back in a few weeks to check that the tablets are working for you.

Do keep this next appointment. There are lots of different types of medications available and those which work for one person do not necessarily help another with similar symptoms.

If you have tried taking the tablets for three or four weeks, without feeling any better, do not make the mistake of delaying returning to see your doctor, thinking that you will never get better, or that tablets are not the answer.

Your doctor may want you to keep on taking the original tablets, or he may feel that there are others which would be more helpful. He will only be able to make the right decision for you, if you keep all your appointments!

There are some people who have severe depression because of some kind of chemical imbalance in the brain. The most important thing is for them to achieve a sense of well-being so that they are able to function in a positive way each day, rather than having fluctuating 'highs' and 'lows' in their moods. Once they have been prescribed the correct medication which helps them balance their mood swings, it is vital that they always remember to keep taking their tablets, rather than only taking them when they feel like it.

Much was written in the media many years ago, about the dangers of anti-depressants becoming addictive, but if you are one of this group of patients, it is essential that, once you have discovered the right medication to help you, **you do not stop** taking it, or reduce the dose, without your doctor agreeing that you do so. Otherwise, you may well go back to 'Square One' and be facing the same battle again with your depression.

Most specialists dealing with patients suffering from depression, seem to agree that the best course of treatment is a mixture of tablets and talking therapies. However, with mental health services stretched to breaking point, there is likely to be a delay of around two months even for an initial assessment. Then, to see a counsellor, there may be an even longer waiting list. If you have been prescribed tablets and referred on for counselling, just because there is a delay, do not decide not to keep your counselling appointment. It may be critical for your long-term recovery, that you have the opportunity to talk things through with someone. Even if you are feeling a bit better by the time your appointment arrives, do not cancel it because, as you talk things through, you may discover what triggered your depression this time and, more importantly, what might help you to prevent another bout of depression in the future.

If you are involved in a Church family, it could be helpful if you talk to your Church minister or house group leader about how you are feeling – at the very least, you would expect him or her to be able to pray that you will get better. He may also be able to give you details of a professionally organised Christian counselling organisation in your area.

If you talk to your minister, you might be pleasantly surprised about how much helpful advice he is able to give you as well as praying for you. However, if you are unable to approach your Church minister and talk to him, or if he seems less than interested or is unwilling to help you through this time, then this is something you may need to think about for the future.

Now is probably not the time to 'jump ship' and look for a different Church. Hopefully, you will have one or two good friends who are part of that Church family you have been involved with and to remove yourself from their friendship, influence and encouragement might not be the best thing for you, while you are recovering from depression.

Above all, do not allow the enemy to plant the thought in your mind that you are unlovable or that this depression (or any other problem in your life) has only happened to you, because God does not love you.

As a Christian you should know already that Jesus came so that you could enjoy life to the full, but you should also be aware that you have an enemy, described in John Chapter 10 verse 10, as a thief who comes only to 'steal and kill and destroy.' Nowhere is the evidence of the devil's handiwork more obvious than in the area of mental health. Recognise that he comes to steal your peace of mind and joy, to kill your hope and sense of purpose and to destroy your faith that God is working things out for your good.

Again in John Chapter 8 verse 44 the Bible talks about the devil being 'a liar and the father of lies.' By his very nature, he will tell you lies – that is his 'mission statement' if you like – from the minute you get up till the minute you go to bed at night, he will try his very best to get you to believe his lies.

He will then try to keep you awake, when you are trying to get to sleep, worrying about all manner of things. Do not be surprised when he tells you things like 'God doesn't love you or this would not be happening to you' or 'you will never get better' or even 'you are hopeless and no-one likes you.'

But as a child of God, you do not have to agree with the devil and his lies. Instead, you must focus on the truth of what God says in His Word and in the completed work of Jesus on the Cross, where he paid the full, total price for you to have complete forgiveness, healing and wholeness.

The whole of Scripture paints a picture of a God who loves you completely and who wants you to be well again.

GOAL

To talk to your Church minister

To see your GP and tell him how you feel

To take your prescribed medication regularly

To have any tests your doctor arranges

To keep any follow up appointments

To write out the first few verses of Psalm 23

Underline the words 'He restores my soul'

CHAPTER 2 WHY DEPRESSION?

That is the million dollar question. You may say 'Why should I feel like this?' (When I have a good job, a nice family, kind friends etc.) The inference is that if you have these factors in your life, then you should somehow be 'immunised' against ever feeling depressed.

Now I'm not saying that you shouldn't be thankful for those people or for the benefits in having a good job. The Bible talks in many places about being thankful for all that God has given us, including homes, food and relationships. Maybe you should take time this week to tell your friends or family how much you appreciate them. You could even tell your boss how much you enjoy working for him! You could also spend the next few moments writing down anything or anyone in your life for which you are thankful.

But, even with all of those things in place, it is still possible to face depression. The truth is that people go through depression for many different reasons. There is never one single event which has caused every kind of depression for every single person, though there may be similar feelings common to most of us. You may have the kind of depression which occurs as a reaction to stressful life events, such as divorce or relationship break-down, illness, moving house, redundancy or bereavement. One person's depression may be triggered by the fact that he now has no work and he had no choice in that decision.

For another person, life was going along smoothly until he was promoted at work. Soon after the family celebrations and congratulations from colleagues were over, the awful reality set in. The new job means three times as much work, 80 emails a day from people chasing up reports and no extra help to achieve the expected results.

Equally, you could have had the kind of upbringing where you were made to feel that you never achieved anything, or that you were not as successful as your older, wiser, better looking, sister. This may not have seemed to cause you too much of a problem as you were growing up (in other words you kept your feelings well hidden, as you were expected to do!) But as time has passed and other life events have conspired to make you feel unworthy, all these earlier feelings may have bubbled up to the surface and caused you to become depressed.

Or you may have had the kind of family which failed to protect you as a child and an older relative or family friend may have 'got away with' abusing you, telling you it was all your fault (which it never is) or that bad things will happen if you ever tell anyone. So you either keep their secret, with the resultant bad feelings hidden deep inside you for as long as you can, or you pluck up the courage to tell someone sometime and risk that the threat of 'bad things' happening will come true.

If you have had to carry this heavy burden with you throughout your childhood and if now as an adult you still feel vulnerable, it is not too late to tell someone about it. Start by telling someone you trust — a family member who was not involved, your Church minister or a caring friend and enlisting their support.

It might surprise you to know that there have been people prosecuted in 2006 who were involved in the sexual abuse of children 20 years ago. They thought they had 'got away with it' but now they have received a long prison sentence and the victims have finally been able to move on and build a more positive future.

If you have been a victim of this kind of abuse, only you know if this is something you can consider revealing many years after the event. If you decide to go ahead and tell someone then you should know that there are many more helpful organisations available to you now than you would have been aware of as a child.

It is almost certain that your story will be believed and that you will not be blamed for whatever took place, even if your abuser was a 'well-respected' member of the community. If you have no-one to confide in, you might want to phone the Samaritans* - even talking to someone who is non-judgemental and confidential might be a valuable experience for you.

There is another group of people who struggle with depression on a regular basis, caused by Seasonal Affected Disorder (S.A.D.) These people 'go downhill', usually when winter comes around, and there are fewer hours of sunshine or bright light which is necessary to produce certain chemical reactions in the brain.

If you can recognise this happening to you most winters, then there are some practical steps you can take, such as buying a 'light box' so that you can sit and read or work in a high degree of bright light for a couple of hours each day.

You could also consider having your main holiday in the winter time. Whilst things are gloomy in February in England, you will discover a whole world of sunshine waiting for you in places such as the Canaries, the Red Sea or the Caribbean – plus winter holidays or flight prices tend to be much cheaper, so you might be able to afford to stay longer.

You may think a holiday in a far away place is an expensive luxury, but you might be pleasantly surprised at how reasonable the price can be, especially if you are able to take advantage of a 'last minute' deal. Also, if every winter the quality of your life is so poor that you barely function, or are unable to do paid work, a holiday break may seem less of a financial liability if it then allows you to carry on with your life for the rest of the year. Viewed even from a 'feel-good' factor alone, a break in the sun may be 'just what the doctor ordered' if you are one of this group of people.

There are other depressed people who may have been raised by the kind of parents who always had a very 'negative' view of life. They may have been unable to make friends easily, and always lived with the feeling that their 'glass is half empty' rather than the more positive view that the 'glass is half full'.

If you have lived through this kind of upbringing, much of this negative thinking will have become embedded in your thought patterns and your approach to life. But you **can unlearn** things, given the right kind of help. The Bible talks in Romans Chapter 12 verse 2, about the possibility of being 'transformed by the renewing of your mind', rather than continuing to live according to the patterns laid down by this world (or even the patterns laid down by your parents).

If you are a Christian, you live by different standards, you have different expectations and a different spirit and, above all, you are in a relationship with the Creator God who is **for you**. He is working things out for you, in spite of how you are feeling right now, for the Scripture says 'we know that in all things God works for the good of those who love him' (Romans Chapter 8 verse 28)

Be careful about the words you use each day, not only about other people, but also about yourself. In Proverbs Chapter 18 verse 21, we read that 'the tongue has the power of life and death.' The negative words you use about your situation can cause your feelings to become even blacker, as you speak.

For instance, if you are approaching enforced and unwelcome retirement from work and you speak to your friends and neighbours on a daily basis about being 'thrown on the scrap-heap' don't be surprised if every day it becomes harder to get out of bed!

A more positive view might be that now you could plan to have some time doing what you want to do, rather than being governed by the alarm clock. You could travel to places you've always wanted to see, or even take up a new hobby. You could ask your Church minister if there is any aspect of your Church's outreach programme that could do with an extra pair of hands. You might even become the one who initiated a new Fairtrade* café at your Church.

Of course, there are people for whom retirement must contain some kind of work, either from a financial or just a practical view-point. The good news is that not all employers take the view that if you're over 50 you're 'over the hill.' Many more enlightened employers are finding out that taking on employees in the 50+ age group, brings a wealth of experience, as well as reliability and good customer care skills.

Current 'anti-ageism' policies presently being implemented, make it illegal for employers to reject older people from employment, purely on age grounds. Hopefully these laws will, in time, mean even more work opportunities for those aged fifty+ who wish to continue working.

So, if work is a necessity for you, make sure you explore all the possibilities out there. Make each day a job-seeking day, whether you approach local DIY stores or consider getting a job as a live-in caring companion in another part of the country.

Before accepting a long term assignment in another part of the country, however, you should check out whether there is a good Church near by and whether you will be able to take time off on Sunday to attend. Some (non Christian) organisations have the idea that Sunday is just another workday and, since Church attendance is not important to them, it should not be an option for you. If you have a tendency towards depression on a regular basis, it will not help you to be out of your usual Church family, with no other means of support nearby.

You could also consider approaching a recruitment agency and applying for 'temp' work. Most agencies, especially those in city centres, need a ready supply of experienced and willing workers on a regular basis. Age is not usually a problem when it comes to temp work – reliability is as important as suitability and older people are often amongst the most reliable members of society.

Whether you are a legal secretary, a fork-lift truck driver or just willing to be a warehouse packer, there is sure to be someone who would welcome your skills. You could register with several agencies and eventually choose to work with the one that is able to offer the regular assignments you enjoy most.

If you are unskilled, you could offer to do voluntary work, whether helping in a charity shop, hospice, hospital or outdoor conservation programme. If working on a paid or voluntary basis does not appeal to you, there is sure to be some kind of group meeting on a regular basis for those over 50 or for those who are interested in the environment or dancing or whatever appeals to you. A visit to your local library might be a good source of information to discover what is happening in your area.

Whatever the reason for your particular state of mind, whether there is a single reason for your depression, or whether it is caused by an accumulation of overwhelming life-events, the main question you ask should not only be 'how did this happen to me?' or even 'how did I get in such a state?' The most important thing is that you allow yourself the opportunity to ask '**how can I get better?**'

As we discovered in Chapter 1, the most important thing is that YOU get the professional help YOU need to discover why YOU are feeling depressed, how YOU can get better and how YOU can help prevent it happening again.

It might help if you keep a diary, writing down your thoughts and feelings about your past, childhood experiences you remember and how you dealt with the different events that happened. When you do eventually get to see a counsellor, you might then have some ideas of the things in your past which caused you distress and how you might best be helped to move on from that in the future.

GOAL

To keep a daily diary

To write down how you feel each day

*Describe any life events and
how you feel about them*

*To keep any counselling appointments, no matter
how long you have been on the waiting list*

*To remind yourself daily of the truth
of Romans Chapter 8 verse 28*

*To write down a list of those things and
people for which you are thankful*

Begin 'Thank you God for........'

CHAPTER 3 DISCOVERING A SENSE OF PURPOSE

As we have already considered in the last Chapter, often people become depressed when their paid employment comes to an end, especially if they had no choice in this matter. Sometimes other people can become depressed because they have no hope for the future and no plans in place. However you may be feeling today, remind yourself that God still has plans for your life!

If you have been depressed for some time and feel overwhelmed with life, it may be that you cannot face getting up and would prefer to stay in bed all day. This is counter-productive as you are already feeling withdrawn from friends and relatives. Removing yourself from all daily routines will give you even less opportunity to engage with people and, whilst you might think this is the right thing to do, staying in bed all day (or staying up for only an hour before 'escaping' to bed for the rest of the day) will **not make you better**!

You need to set realistic goals for getting up in a morning and eventually for getting out and about and getting on with your life. If you feel burnt out and have taken to staying in bed all day, do not set yourself an impossible target like getting up at 6 am. and staying up till 11pm.

Instead, set your alarm clock for maybe 10 am. (and then **get up**). If you can set your C.D. player on 'timed' to play your favourite piece of music, so much the better. Otherwise, find a piece of music which inspires you and play it first of all, as part of your morning routine.

Then, take a shower, using whatever shower gel most helps you 'feel alive'. Even if you have traditionally preferred a bath, take a shower, as this will help you to clear your mind and feel refreshed, whereas a bath will probably help you relax and go to sleep (you have already been doing too much of that, remember!)

Even if you haven't felt like being around people recently, at least if you are up, you may have the opportunity to speak with the postman, or meter reader, or catalogue delivery driver. (Yes, you may also run into the double glazing salesman, but that's real life, I'm afraid!)

Use each of the people who come to your door, as an opportunity for you to engage in conversation with someone. Even if you can only talk about the weather in week one, perhaps by week four you may be able to chat more easily and might even be ready to face friends or relatives.

Begin each day with a regular time of prayer and reading God's Word. If you use a particular set of daily reading notes that you have always found helpful, take time to read them. If you have never used daily readings before, can we suggest trying 'Word For Today' from United Christian Broadcasters?* This is helpful and up to date and is encouraging, whether you have been a Christian for many years or even if you are a new believer.

As you begin your prayer time, ask God to fill you with His Holy Spirit and to reveal new things from His Word as you read your

Bible. Do not worry if you cannot remember what you have read, it may still take root in your heart and mind. Whatever the enemy whispers to you, this time is valuable and it is certainly **not** a waste of time. You could even write out one special verse and stick it on the fridge or somewhere else so that you can see it during the day.

You could maybe take a short walk – if you have a dog, you might go for a longer walk. If you do not have a dog of your own, borrow a friend's or, better still, offer to walk a dog belonging to a neighbour or an older person in your street. They will probably be pleased you offered and you would at least have had more opportunities to talk with someone than you had yesterday, when all you did was stay in bed.

If you have managed to stay up all morning, after lunch, you may then give yourself permission to take a nap (maximum one hour). After another short walk, you might feel like making a quick visit to the supermarket. If the thought of this brings on a panic attack, try a visit to the library, or the local corner shop. Do not shut yourself away all day. Try to visit or phone friends after tea, before going to bed at 10.00 pm.

If you are able to re-programme your body clock in this way, when you realise that you can survive getting up, after four weeks you could start to get out of bed slightly earlier and go to bed at night at a more normal time – so that even having a social life becomes a distinct possibility. If you used to meet in a Church house group or similar time of fellowship, aim to return as soon as you can. If that seems a daunting prospect, perhaps you could ask the leader if he will meet you half way, so that you could arrive together.

Every few months, look again at the balance of your life. Does each week include:

- Time to worship God
- Opportunities to meet with other people
- Times to relax, alone
- Opportunities to serve others without any financial reward
- Fun times when you can enjoy your favourite hobby or interest
- Regular times of exercise or sport
- Opportunity for some kind of paid work
  (unless you are happily retired)

Finding something purposeful to do is important for all of us, no matter at what stage of life we are. At least one politician has recognised (yes we know it was a long time coming!) that everything in life doesn't have to be about how much money we can accumulate. If that were the only issue, then there would be no depressed millionaires or lottery winners.

We have already discussed that approaching retirement can be a trigger for depression for some people, because they have only achieved a sense of purpose in their daily work. But these feelings of life being pointless can affect younger people, too.

Students can feel overwhelmed with exams, their own (or

parents) expectations, fear of failure, or fear of being unable to find a suitable job at the end of four years study, even with a sparkling set of exam results.

Every year the newspapers carry reports of suicides amongst the young, usually the very brightest, often very caring young people. As a society, what kind of world are we creating if even those who have already achieved much do not feel at ease?

What a waste of talent, potential and resources are represented by these statistics. But, of course, these young people are not simply statistics, they are usually much loved, highly valued (but maybe no-one bothered to tell them how highly they were valued) and above all, they are someone's son or daughter.

Parents, what kind of message are you giving to your child? Take a few minutes to consider the foundations you have laid for them. Did your desire to see them enrol at a grammar school push your son into extra tuition, even before he took the 11-plus or entrance exam?

Did you brainwash them from an early age with the truth that 'everyone in our family goes to university'? Or, if you come from a mining community in Yorkshire, did you tell your son that 'we never went to university, we went down the pit when we were 15 and now you just need to get a job and pay us back for all we've given you.'

Just as unrealistic expectations can lay a foundation for future depression in our young people, so too, can the overwhelming feeling that they were never able to fulfil their potential in the way that was appropriate to them.

If we have young people in our family, about to take exams, we need to remind them that we will still love them, whatever their results. If we have young people who do not have an academic mind-set, we owe it them to help them explore all career options and then to take the steps necessary to 'follow their dream'. Of course, if they are following the Lord, then we also need to encourage them to seek His guidance regarding His choice of future career and to reassure them that God has a wonderful plan for their lives and yours.

But, above all, we need to learn to listen, really listen to our young people. After all, it **is their life**. They did not ask to be born; they do not owe us anything. Of course we would like them to be grateful for the love and care we've given them for many years. But we dare not live our lives through them, even in the misguided attempt to 'give them the opportunities we never had.'

The best route to success is not always a grammar school for every young boy. Some young people would be far better being in the top set in an excellent comprehensive school, rather than always being in the bottom of a group of highly academic pupils at a grammar or private school.

A university course may be right for some girls, but others may prefer to work for a bank or building society or an engineering company who will pay them while they work and also pay for them to attend day release at college. At the end of three years they will not only have a career, but they may finish with a qualification equivalent to a degree, and all achieved without any student debt!

In these times of considerable pressure, young people do not need the added burden of not only finding their own way in life, but also feeling that they have to fulfil their parents expectations, otherwise they will be branded a 'failure.'

What about other mile-stones in life that can affect young people? It seems to me less than helpful for the Government to engage in a programme of installing contraceptive machines in schools as a way of preventing teenage pregnancies.

Whilst we know that there are a small minority of people who choose to sleep around, most young people I know want to get on with their lives without the added peer pressure to sleep with the current boyfriend just because others are doing so. They are often just as aware as you are of the mechanics of how everything works!

The last thing they need is a machine in the school cloakroom reminding them that the adults around here expect them to have very little in the way of moral values or even sound judgement.

Our Christian teenagers need the support of an encouraging and inspiring youth worker, bringing sound Biblical teaching on the importance of waiting for marriage before getting involved in a sexual relationship. If your Church has a youth minister, pray for him. If not, pray for the team responsible for the youth work and do everything in your power to encourage them, as they work in this rewarding, but often time consuming mission field.

What if, in spite of your prayers and sound teaching, things go wrong? What about those for whom it all goes 'pear shaped?' (Literally!) Whenever a young girl gets pregnant at the 'wrong' time in her life, there is bound to be a lot of soul-searching. But let's remember that apart from the disappointed 'older and wiser' parents, there are three very important people here: the mum to be, the father to be and the not yet welcomed baby. Again, we need to listen to the young people who are currently trying to work through the most traumatic news they have ever received.

The health care professionals or even some parents of the teenagers involved, may be of the opinion that an abortion is the only way out and may seek to affirm that having a baby will 'ruin your life.' But again, this is another time that the young people themselves need to be assured that, not only will we continue to love them, but that we will also stand by them and support them in their decision making.

I know many young girls who had a baby when they were not planning one and they are generally doing an excellent job of raising their child, with ongoing help from family and friends. For them to have been pushed into an abortion to suit their parents, would not only have been morally indefensible, but might also have triggered depression later in life. Far from 'getting rid' of the problem, these girls might have realised that, as well as making an initial 'mistake' in getting pregnant, they have only compounded the problem by adding a lifetime of guilt over allowing or arranging the killing of their unborn baby.

Nowhere has the work of the enemy been more obvious than in the issue of abortion. It is time for Christians to be brave enough to raise awareness that, instead of abortion, there are other options to be considered. These days, thankfully, no one sends their daughters away to the country, or to a convent to have their baby and save their parents 'sense of shame'.

These days, the girl could first of all decide to go ahead with the pregnancy and have the baby. She might then, later decide to arrange for the baby to be adopted and there would be no shortage of caring people who are unable to have children of their own, who would be thankful to be entrusted with this new life.

If, however, the girl decides to keep the baby and pursue a career, there are more support networks available than ever before. I know girls who have gone to university, or teacher training college where child care was provided, or courses deferred for part of a year, or where older family members cared for the new baby, whilst the girl continued to study for her degree.

After the initial shock of an unplanned pregnancy, the new

grandparents are often amongst those who celebrate with great joy the arrival of this new baby and then celebrate all over again at their daughter's graduation ceremony.

If you are a young girl reading this and you have recently discovered that you are pregnant, even if you do not think your family will be supportive, they might just surprise you! **Make sure you tell someone as soon as you can**. If you can't face your parents alone, take a friend, teacher, or church youth worker with you. You owe it to yourself to **make sure your views are listened to** and that you are not pushed into a decision you might later regret.

If your parents turn out to be amongst the very few that are not helpful, you will find that there are lots of people out there who will be very supportive. There are caring people in well established organisations* who will literally be a life-line for you. They will have heard many stories like yours before and they will know how to help you.

Then, there are young and these days, not so young, mothers who can find themselves in the midst of post-natal depression which crept up on them with the arrival of a new baby. The combination of little sleep and a huge amount of house-work which feels as big as 'painting the Forth Bridge' all comes at a time when the hormones are out of balance, after pregnancy and childbirth.

Instead of thinking 'I can't tell anyone how I'm feeling – I have a new baby to look after, and I simply can't cope'! You should enlist the help of your health visitor. Hopefully you have already established a caring relationship with her. Over the past few years, she will have heard from many other mums who feel exactly as you do and is sure to know how to help you. It could be that you need some medication from your GP to help restore a sense of equilibrium. But it may be that you are feeling depressed because your life has changed in a way for which you were ill prepared.

Look at your expectations of yourself. It simply isn't possible to look after the (important) needs of a new baby and do every bit of (not so important) dusting, gardening and ironing, just as you did before.

You should ignore anything that isn't absolutely necessary (birth congratulations cards will cover most surfaces needing dusting in the first few days anyway!) Welcome the help offered by friends, family or consider paying professional cleaners, even if only for a few hours or a few weeks.

Without turning this into a parentcraft manual, there is not space to look at all the issues surrounding post-natal depression, but there are excellent publications around, from books at the library to monthly magazines at the supermarket. They all give valuable advice and do not forget the importance of having a support network around you, whether from other mums you meet at the clinic, library or your Church or community based parent & toddler group.

If you have begun keeping a diary each day, describing how you feel today, you might also wish to add any positive things you have done for that day and what you plan to do tomorrow.

Even something as basic as a 'To Do' list can be turned into a positive experience, if you start the day with a list of six things and are able to tick off four of them as completed tasks, with two more on the way to being achievable by the end of the week.

Do make sure your list is **realistic**, though, or you will end up feeling even worse than you do at this moment. For instance, achieving Grade III in violin playing might be an unattainable goal, if you have never progressed beyond playing 'Twinkle, twinkle, little star!'

If you have not vacuumed the house for three weeks, because you feel so depressed, putting 'Spring Clean the Whole House!' at the top of your list will only serve to make you rush back to bed, feeling soul-destroyed.

On the other hand, if you break down each job into small tasks, you may be surprised by what you have managed to do by the week-end. The 'whole bathroom cleaned' could seem like an impossible dream, but you might be able to clean the sink today, the bath tomorrow and the toilet the next day.

Tackling the whole ironing basket might feel like a mountain to climb, it might even begin to **look like a mountain**, but if you tackle a few items each day, you might yet see the bottom of the laundry basket by the end of the week (or month, or year!)

Depending on whether or not you are running for 'housewife (or husband) of the year' you might also want to try this tip:

After taking jumpers, shirts or T-shirts out of the washing machine, dry them individually on coat hangers. They will need very little ironing.

Tell teenagers who reach 15 (or whatever age you decide is not cruel) that they are going to do their own ironing from now on. Yes, we know they will pull a funny face, declare that life is not fair and that 'Kevin's Mum' does all his ironing. But they (and you) might just survive!

If you promise not to report me to the 'authorities', I can tell you that I have tried this approach with at least two teenage boys and it worked. They somehow also discovered that when you take a T-shirt off the coat hanger, it doesn't even need ironing. Magic!

In the beginning, if the boys moaned or pulled a funny face, I reminded them that some day, some girl would thank me that I had at least produced the man she married who knew how to iron his own clothes! (Send the flowers now, girls!)

We have already considered that some tasks we set ourselves are not really necessary, or at least not essential, when viewed in the light of the sometimes overwhelming work involved in caring for a new baby. We may have allowed ourselves to unwittingly be brainwashed with the idea that 'if you want a job doing, do it yourself'! If you insist on doing every job yourself, do not be surprised if you are exhausted by the end of the week.

You could instead, involve your partner, older children or extended family. Even the visitor who called to welcome your new baby would surely not mind you asking 'please could you put the kettle on and make a cup of tea and then we can catch up on what's happening in the world'!

With the arrival of a new baby, you have moved from maybe being a manager at work to now being the full time manager at home (even if this is only for a short while.) You will survive and complete this assignment successfully, if you learn to delegate.

There are some jobs which only you can do, but there are other jobs which may not be done in exactly the same way by someone else, but they will get done, nevertheless. You could still all be alive tomorrow, if you allow your husband to make the dinner. Okay, so his gravy might be lumpier than yours, but you might even discover that he is a better cook than you – (alright, so you already know where this is leading!)

Along with delegating tasks to others, do not forget that you can now order all your shopping on-line. The first time I did it, I confess it took me half an hour to progress beyond ordering the milk. But the second time I was much faster and I can now order a weeks shopping in that time. Best of all, I get to sit with a well-deserved coffee, while the man with the van trudges up my path through the snow, with all my heavy shopping, is that smart or what?

Finally, do make sure that you reward yourself for every job well-done. After you've tackled a pile of ironing, consider having a 15-minute break listening to your favourite music. On a sunny day, if you decide to weed the garden, when you've done as much as you can face, sit down and enjoy half an hour on your neat and tidy patch of grass.

As an old poet once remarked, 'What is this life if, full of care, we have no time to stand and stare?' Adopt this poem as your new daily rule!

Decide what is right for you, whether it's having some 'me time' alone, an evening dinner with your partner while his Mother baby sits, or just having a new hairstyle.

If money is an issue you might find that your local college hair and beauty department will book you in for a haircut, manicure or massage for a fraction of the high street price.

If you haven't got a pound or two to spare to treat yourself to a new blouse once in a while, consider this: I once saved enough money for a holiday for two abroad, just by economising over the previous six months. I always was a frugal shopper, but now, with a holiday in the sun beckoning, I became a 'woman on a mission'.

I listed everything I spent, especially on the weekly supermarket shop and decided to try and save £20 off that bill every week. I took special note of the 'buy one get one free' offers. The best part of this whole exercise? (apart from the actual holiday) nobody in my family noticed any difference in the food we ate!

If you are trying to economise, as your baby grows, you might also have items of baby clothes or furniture you no longer need. You could advertise them for sale, or even persuade your partner to do a car boot sale — ask relatives if they have any items in the garage they no longer use. For one morning of enjoyable work, you could have enough cash for a whole weekend away in a nice hotel, being pampered.

Look at the balance of your life and check that each work task achieved is met with some type of reward. This does not need to be a box or even a bar of chocolate — for you it might be more helpful to take a stroll around the park on a sunny day.

In most workplace situations, whenever a sales target is reached or a successful 'Ofsted' report is achieved, the staff involved might be given a cash bonus or be taken out for a meal. If you have perhaps given up paid work for a while to devote yourself to your new baby, it is even more vital to your sense of well-being, that you feel valued and that all your hard work is recognised.

Do not think of this as a luxury — after all, if you were not caring so well for your baby, he or she might be spending all day in a nursery or some other form of paid childcare, which would eat away a large chunk of your household income.

GOAL

To get up earlier each day

*To look objectively at **realistic** expectations of yourself*

*Adding to the diary a 'To Do' list each day, **deciding** which tasks are priorities*

*Check and delete any tasks **not necessary***

***Delegate** any suitable jobs to other people*

*To tick off each task as you finish and **reward** yourself for a job **well done!***

*To read again **Jeremiah Chapter 29 verse 11** remembering that God still has plans for your life*

CHAPTER 4 SEX, MYTHS AND DOWNRIGHT LIES

Having looked in the previous chapter at issues surrounding the arrival of a new baby, this leads us into the whole area of sex, fulfilment and loving relationships.

If you were to pick up a copy of most tabloid newspapers you could be forgiven for thinking that the whole of life is dominated by sex. Advertisers are born, it would seem, already programmed with the idea that 'sex sells' so we have the typical scenario at the motor show where the 'must have' new car has to appeal to men's sexual preferences. This is underlined by the fact that it comes complete with a scantily dressed female draped provocatively over the car bonnet - in the photo shoot at least, even if that imagery is far removed from everyday life in your experience.

Then again, most films or plays have the idea weaving throughout the plot that most normal young people are 'diving between the sheets' with every boyfriend at the end of a first date, whilst the notion that their mums and dads might be 'at it' is laughable, or at least downright embarrassing!

So, let us explode some of the myths and bring some sanity back into the sexual arena. Sex is a part of life, just as eating and drinking (and shopping and working) are also a part of normal life. Whilst most people would agree that sex represents a more delicious part of life than cleaning the oven, or even digging the garden, proper time and space need to be given to all these activities, if life is to retain its fragile balance.

Past generations had the idea that God, or at least the Church, thinks sex is bad, certainly not enjoyable and only allowed if each act results in procreation. In spite of false teaching to the contrary, that idea is not represented in Scripture, where sexual fulfilment is portrayed as the gift of a loving God to His children, to be enjoyed within a marriage relationship, consisting of one man and one woman for life.

Though there are many 'in depth' books written from a Scriptural point of view on this subject, even looking briefly at the fifth Chapter of Ephesians will remind us that sex is very much God's idea, that the right emphasis on the sexual act is not sexual avoidance, nor sexual immorality, but the 'one flesh' experience highlighted within the marriage service.

When young people are taught nothing about rightful sexual expression within marriage, about the possibility of waiting for this union with the right person at the right time, we make it easy for them to fall into the trap that 'any date will do'. When older people have the idea that it is ok to walk out on a marriage and children for the guy next door, or even the hotel waiter in Morocco, it is certain that their immorality will have a lasting effect, if not on the adults involved, most certainly on their children and rejected spouse.

Most people who give in to the temptation to stray from their marriage vows, do not set out deliberately to betray their husband or wife, with the notion that they are going to find out how it feels to sleep with Mary next door or Fred the Church warden. Usually, some ingredient is missing or neglected within their marriage and they are tempted by loving concern, or whispered intimacy from an inappropriate acquaintance, whether at work, Church or in the neighbourhood.

The wife who feels undervalued at home, is an easy target for someone else to come along and remind her how caring and sensitive she is. The next door neighbour might not use the words 'my wife doesn't understand me', but he can make it almost believable that you and he deserve each other, if your present spouse does not value emotional intimacy. The husband who works long hours in a strenuous job might become vulnerable to alternative expressions of love, even if he knows they are wrong, if he has a wife who has no time for anything but the children and housework, or who makes it clear that she is never going to be available or interested in a fulfilling sex life.

Before the opportunity arises for you to become tempted to stray outside of your marriage, if there are areas of concern, would it not be in your best interests to address those issues which make you feel neglected or unloved? Perhaps you could explore the possibility of attending an Alpha marriage course* or even reading the Alpha marriage course manual. Session 6 of the manual is a whole chapter devoted to good sex!

A final area which needs mentioning, is that confusion over their sexual identity is a problem for some people. The natural questioning and surrounding confusion, especially for some teenage boys, has not been helped by media intrusion of certain celebrities.

It is perhaps not so surprising that some people with questions are afraid to address their concerns to anyone with authority, a factor which could lead them into depression. The strident voices of a minority of homosexual men have done little to clear the truth from the myth. For instance, we are regularly told that around one in five men have homosexual tendencies. Unfortunately, these erroneous statistics may be welcomed by those who are on a crusade to persuade us all that being gay is a great lifestyle choice.

The truth is that there are far fewer homosexual men than these people would have us believe. In fact, in our street of over a hundred houses, populated by around two hundred or so men, I do not know of one single gay man (or lesbian woman, for that matter.) If you think about your own area, I would suggest that the figures are pretty similar. Whereas if the erroneous statistics were believable, either in your house or your neighbours houses, there would have to be at least one gay man or woman, wouldn't there? The other issue often raised, but not supported by the Bible, is that these men can't help it, they are just born homosexuals. Unfortunately this label is applied equally to men who have just 'discovered' their homosexuality, even after being involved in heterosexual relationships, having married and fathered and raised children. Of course these issues need to be discussed in greater detail than this book will allow, but what is interesting is that some men considered they were born heterosexual, until they explored the possibilities and experimented with homosexual practices and then came to the conclusion that they were, after all, 'born homosexual'.

I have even heard men in just this category who, after their marriage had ended for whatever reason, having taken themselves off to the local town's 'gay village' were surprised to be approached by a homosexual man and thereafter concluded that this new partner was sent by God, confirming that they were, after all 'born gay'.

I do not believe that the Bible supports this theory. I believe God gives us free will and that when men or women give in to temptation, explore and experiment with homosexual practices and experiences, these can become acceptable and part of their 'normal' behaviour. They can then go on to defend their behaviour choice and even present us with their own version of the Bible, which seems, to them at least, to endorse their lifestyle choice as righteous.

Whilst this would have been unthinkable many years ago, this has now become so acceptable that some Churches have welcomed homosexual ministers and proclaimed their views to be Scriptural.

Whilst never doubting the need for compassion for all those involved, as Christians our main focus must surely be to submit to God's authority as revealed in His Word, on all these matters.

If this is an area of concern for you or your family members, we would suggest you contact 'True Freedom Trust'* which has been set up to help present a balanced and honest picture, in accordance with Scripture. Having been established many years ago, by those who came out of a homosexual lifestyle, they are able to offer support and counselling if you feel this would be helpful.

Before concluding this chapter on sex and the choices you and I make in life and relationships, right choices are just as vital in heterosexual relationships. Within the last few months, I have read about those who destroyed their own marriage and a loving family belonging to someone else when they decide to recreate their fantasy from school days and become reunited with an old schoolfriend via the internet.

After the initial passion has reached beyond the so called 'honeymoon' stage and the excitement of clandestine meetings, even if this fantasy works out (which could be highly unlikely) your new relationship will still require commitment and hard work – the same ingredients you needed in your present 'boring' marriage!

I even heard one guy being interviewed recently on television, explaining that his adultery is excusable because it actually saves his marriage from divorce (this last scenario made me want to phone in to the television station and asked if this man had ever heard of 'flying pigs'). The uncomfortable truth which he could possibly be about to discover in the coming days is that, whilst he might not have consulted a divorce lawyer, nor signed the divorce papers – in his head or maybe his heart he has divorced himself (emotionally if not physically) from his current marriage partner. Each act of sexual union with his new lover will release hormones in both of them which enforce the bonding process (similar to the bonding process enjoyed by a mother and her new baby) and he might yet have cause to regret his act of betrayal when viewed through his wife's or his children's eyes in a future filled with sadness.

If you are reading this, I want to say to you, before your sanity deserts you and the moment of madness turns into a lifetime of foolishness, think of this: that same television producer may not be so keen to do a re-run of the programme, after your marriage has fallen apart, when you are only allowed limited access to your children. Instead of directing all your energies into an illicit affair or long term adulterous relationship, if, instead you obtained the right help and channelled your energies into your existing marriage, you may yet see future excitement and passion, where presently you can only see boredom. Your children may, in the future, have cause to thank you that they, at least, did not have to go through the nightmare of a broken home and a yo-yo childhood, as they were shared between two warring parents.

GOAL

To read Ephesians Chapter 5 verses 1 – 4
(The Message translation is great!)

To consider the phrase 'extravagant'
love and aim to love like that

If single, check when and how
you last met new people

Do you need to seek ways of creating
new loving relationships?

Beware of starting each day in the same old rut

If married make time to enrich your marriage

Explore ways of having a happy and healthy sex life

Make plans to attend an Alpha marriage course

If you are facing marriage difficulties,
arrange to have some kind of counselling

Do not settle for less than the best!

CHAPTER 5 HEALTHY EATING

If you are feeling depressed with little motivation to get up, it may seem impossible to feel like eating, much less to prepare anything to eat. The truth (which you will not want to hear) is that you will not get better if all you eat is noodle and hot water prepared in 30 seconds, using only a kettle. That might do **occasionally** for a student on the go, but it will not help you as a lifestyle choice if that's all you are eating Monday to Friday and you really want to get better.

Medical experts worldwide are convinced that for maximum health, we need to emphasise the importance of good nutrition. A healthy diet should bring a balance of protein, carbohydrate, fibre, fruit and vegetables, vitamins and minerals, with less than we have been used to of salt, sugar and fat. The truth is, if you have got into the habit of eating at 'fast food' outlets or even buying convenient ready made meals, off the supermarket shelf, these are the products which usually have the highest concentration of salt, sugar and fats.

You may feel ill now, but if these have become your only menu, you may soon be adding obesity or heart problems to your health concerns about your depression. Over the next seven days, keep a food diary. Starting with breakfast, write down everything you eat. Make sure you include snacks and drinks and always ensure that you drink enough water, rather than fizzy canned drinks.

Take one meal at a time and find out how much each part of that meal has cost and how much sugar, salt and fat it contains. Then see if you can substitute any part of it with a healthier choice. Remember, not everything you eat has to be cooked – eating a banana as a snack might be much better for you than having a handful of chocolate biscuits. If you are feeling ill and the thought of cooking a big meal seems overwhelming, try boiling or poaching an egg, with wholemeal toast, instead of reaching for that easy option, plastic pot of noodles.

If cooking healthy food seems like a foreign language to you, consider enrolling on a college cookery course - you never know, you might just end up with a whole new set of friends or even a career out of it!

In the meantime, look at the meals you do prepare – what do they look like on the plate? For instance, if you prepare your food with little thought, you could just serve up white chicken, mashed potato and cauliflower - a very bland and uninspiring meal.

If, instead, you add to the chicken portion a healthy salad, using green lettuce, cress, cucumber, red tomatoes, celery, red pepper, beetroot, coleslaw and a spoonful of sweetcorn, your plate has become much more colourful and more desirable to eat.

During their training, professional chefs are taught that we eat first 'with our eyes'. In other words, if the food looks attractive, we will be enthusiastic about eating it. Every time you prepare a meal, ask yourself the question 'how could I make this meal look better'? Even just a sprinkle of chopped chives, fresh parsley and a slice of tomato will add to the appearance of humble cottage pie. If you have no garden, you could still grow a pot of your favourite herbs on the kitchen windowsill.

Of course, it is easy to suggest adding six items to your plate, as a way of making your food more exciting, but extra shopping does not come free. If money is in short supply, you might consider sharing the cost of these extra items with a friend, or even sharing mealtimes with a friend, taking it in turns to provide the food and cook a main meal each day.

The early Church emphasised the value of sharing together, including eating together. Whilst eating together was not the only reason they experienced such phenomenal numerical growth, if it was important then, you can be sure that it is still important today. You may need to consider whether you and your Church create opportunities for this to happen on a regular basis. Apart from the spiritual implications, solely on a practical basis, it takes considerable effort to prepare and then eat every meal alone.

By involving others, not only is the mealtime shared, becoming much more stimulating, but, in addition, the cost of a shared shopping trip could be halved or at least, reduced.

Also, there are certain times of the day when supermarkets reduce the prices on items they need to sell quickly. On Sunday afternoons and many evenings around 8pm, some supermarkets put whole racks of products on sale at the entrance foyer, often at a fraction of their usual price. This might be a good way for you to experiment with different foods which are normally out of your price range.

As well as looking at the food you eat and its preparation, you should also plan to include some form of exercise each day. At the beginning, this may only consist of gentle walking, but at least it is more positive than simply retreating to your bed each day. In time you might want to consider joining an exercise class – your GP might also be able to suggest 'exercise on prescription' and send you to a local fitness centre at a reduced charge. This would have the added bonus of allowing you to talk to other people, as well as getting daily exercise. It is well known that exercise releases 'feel good' hormones and, whilst this may not immediately be apparent, it is worth persevering with your exercise plan.

When you feel able to tackle more than gentle walking, you might also want to join a serious walking or rambling club – your tourist board, library or newspaper might know of such a group in your area. If you can pluck up the courage to consider joining, phone the secretary first, explain that you'll be coming on your own and ask if they have any advice for you as a novice. Usually any organiser worth their salt will be keen to encourage new members and will probably make a great effort to welcome you into the group.

Exercise will only work for you, if you choose an activity you enjoy and you make the time to fit it into your daily schedule. A busy mum might not have the time each day to join a gym, but she could perhaps buy a 'side stepping' machine and use that to exercise each day, whilst listening to some upbeat music. If you do not enjoy walking or bike riding, a swimming class might be more your thing. To help lift your mood, though, your exercise would be best if it also contains an element of meeting other people and having the opportunity to talk to them.

Relaxation exercises might also help you to feel calm and less stressed. Your local health centre might provide relaxation classes which you could attend. Your library would usually have books on relaxation techniques. These typically involve listening to soothing music, whilst you imagine you are lying on some tropical beach as you adopt a steady, controlled, breathing pattern.

Again, consider that for you, there might be more value in joining a class of other people rather than simply doing the exercises alone every day. For the Christian, it might be helpful to avoid those meditation techniques which rely on Eastern religions or ritual chanting.

Having considered that what you eat may well have an effect on your mood, if you are vegetarian, you should also check that your diet gives you an adequate supply of vitamins and minerals. Ask to be referred to a hospital dietician, if you think you may need help with this or if you know that you are overweight. Just ignoring a weight issue will not make it go away and professional help to achieve a gradual weight loss, combined with exercise will be much better than a life of 'yo-yo' dieting.

As well as looking at the importance of what we eat, there are other factors which could have an effect on those who are depressed. It has long been documented that, around the time of the menopause, hormone levels for women can fluctuate, leading to mood swings, anxiety and depression, as well as hot flushes during the day and night. If these symptoms are a problem for you, your doctor should be able to suggest ways of helping you cope with this or might possibly refer you to a specialist for more expert care.

Although these difficulties have been recognised as a factor in the health of women, very little importance has traditionally been attached to men's hormone levels in mid to later life. There may be some men who need blood tests to establish whether they have decreased levels of testosterone, which could be affecting their ability to function. It is usually understood that normal levels of testosterone are required for healthy sexual function, but other side effects of low testosterone can include anxiety, depression and memory loss, as well as reduced muscle density and weight loss. If you have been suffering from depression for some time, without relief in spite of taking the anti-depressants suggested by your doctor, you might want to ask if he could arrange a blood test, or refer you to a consultant who would be able to check your level of testosterone and, if it is found to be reduced, suggest the most appropriate treatment.

Before ending this chapter on healthy eating, we should mention briefly that there are some people for whom their depression is also linked to other eating disorders such as anorexia or bulimia. Whilst the reasons for such eating disorders are often very complex, one thing is common – there is usually a great attempt made by the sufferer to cover up this aspect of their behaviour. Perhaps they sit down to a meal with the family, but spend the whole time pushing the food around their plate. Or they may eat normally, only to disappear to the toilet soon after to make themselves sick or take laxatives.

If this destructive pattern of behaviour is a problem for you, do not cover it up any longer. You owe it to yourself to have a full and satisfying life, one that is not controlled or dominated by food or the size of your waist. If you contact your doctor, being honest about what is happening to you and your controlling behaviour through food, he is sure to be able to arrange expert help for you.

There are also specialist books* written, as well as Christian Healing Centres* which make an effort to help those with eating disorders.

The longer you conceal the reality of your situation, the more life is passing you by. You have been created to have a full and positive life, do not accept anything less for one day longer.

GOAL

To keep a daily food diary making a note of everything you eat and drink each day

To learn new recipes or cooking skills

To enjoy some kind of daily exercise

To get expert help for any kind of eating disorder

To read Acts Chapter 2 verses 42 - 47

CHAPTER 6 BAD OR MAD ?

We have already looked at the fact that people suffering from depression can have low self esteem. Because of the way they were raised, they can have an overwhelming feeling that they are unworthy of enjoying life or normal relationships. They can have irrational thoughts that they are 'too bad' to be considered worthwhile.

They may have been told so often that they are 'thick' whilst at school, that they never attempted to learn any new skills. If they had been at school in more recent times, a teacher may have discovered that, far from being unintelligent, they were maybe suffering from dyslexia or some other learning difficulty, which could have been overcome, given the right help.

Whilst the whole of Scripture points to the fact that God loves you just as you are, He also wants you to achieve your full potential. If you feel that you missed out on educational opportunities when young, it is not too late to learn new skills. Consider evening classes at college, or enrolling on an Open University course.

If formal education is not for you, simply set yourself a task and do your own research. You could think of a country you have never visited, try and learn some of the language; find out about the people and their culture, as well as learning about the food most commonly eaten in that region. Try out some recipes, then, when you are feeling better, you might reward yourself with a visit to that place. Work out how you can raise the money to fund your trip. Or at least pray for the country and those Christian missions working there. Make this project your goal for the next three months.

People who are depressed can also have the problem, caused by anxiety or stress, that they are unable to remember things. The thought uppermost in their minds can be 'If I can't remember things, I must be going mad'.

Before giving much room to the thought of early dementia setting in, let us look objectively at what is happening here. If someone has been suffering from depression for a while, he or she usually has little interest in their surroundings or even what is going on the world at large. The depression may have been growing over a period of time, during which time they have been gradually withdrawing from life and from taking part in conversations.

Because they now have little interest in life, they feel unable to 'take anything in'. They can have problems concentrating on the thing that was discussed five minutes ago, never mind events from yesterday.

If you are unable to concentrate at this moment in time, it stands to reason that you would have difficulty remembering things from yesterday – the truth is that you were probably only 'half listening' at the time. Instead of worrying about the possibility of the early onset of dementia, just **accept** that you have a mind overcrowded with anxious thoughts just now and that you are struggling to hang on to anything extra **at this moment in time**. Accept that this is a passing state of mind – when you recover from this depression, you will once again be able to remember.

Having accepted that this is a temporary phase and that your normal memory will return, once you are back to your old self, what can you do, until you get better?

Write things down if they are important. In an earlier chapter we discussed writing a 'To Do' list. If you have already taken that advice on board, it should now have become second nature to you. If you are asked to cook tea, write down a list of ingredients you will need to buy, along with the oven temperature and cooking times.

You might feel childish writing things down, but the truth is that if you asked the most successful business leaders in the country, how they manage to achieve so much, I expect you will find that every one of them writes down things they consider to be important for each day.

Involve your partner, friend, or family member in playing a popular word game. As well as giving you the chance to make up words and add up scores, if you have been withdrawn recently this could help with conversation. Simply chatting about whether your opponent's word is allowed or laughing together when you spell a word incorrectly, will have the added bonus of preventing you from keep going over the same old anxious thoughts, at least for a little while. Set a time limit of an hour to play the game – this is supposed to be fun, not a marathon!

Above all, do not keep using the same old negative words, even in jest. If you keep saying 'I must be going round the bend' or 'I really am losing my marbles' these words will merely serve to reinforce your old patterns of thinking. Each day you will then wake up even more convinced that you really are 'losing the plot!'

You are instead now on the road to recovery, adopting new thoughts about yourself, on the way to achieving new goals each day. In any case, you will discover that the people you most admire, who may be holding down a prominent job in your community, can all have an 'off day' when they forget someone's name at a dinner party or turn up late for a meeting because they forgot the start time.

The only difference is, they will usually dismiss it with a laugh, entertain others over dinner with the amusing thought that they were 'having a senior moment!' whilst you beat yourself up for your every failure. Be generous to yourself, forgive your mistakes.

In spite of your mistakes, Jesus is **still** the Redeemer. That picture of Him will have been indelibly written on your heart in those first days of your salvation and commitment to Him in a new covenant. Now you need to allow yourself a time of reflection as you remember that He is also able to redeem your current situation. What is the point of knowing a God who has forgiven you, if you are unable to forgive yourself?

Whilst you will certainly have good days and bad days, do not emphasise your small, usually insignificant failings and do not underestimate all the good things you have done. If you have made a mistake, recognise it and then move on. Do not allow it to take root in your mind and prevent you attempting another assignment.

You are not useless, no matter how overburdened you were feeling when you first picked up this book. When you are feeling fully fit (or maybe even before then) you will find something you enjoy doing and you will be able to do it successfully. Your aim should be to build healthy relationships – not to continue living in isolation.

If you have spent the last six months shutting yourself away from friends, if you have stopped returning phone calls when relatives rang to talk to you, you need to gradually pick up the threads of life again. It will not be easy, but you do have to begin reconnecting with people. Think of the person you find easiest to talk to and make contact with them.

You could start by phoning them. Begin with a simple apology: 'I'm so sorry, I didn't call you back. I've been feeling ill for the last 6 months, but I'm on new tablets now and feeling a bit better. Anyway, that's enough about me, what have you been up to?' Then you could finish your phone call by asking if you could call round to see them next week and arranging a suitable time.

Having arranged a time to visit, make sure you keep to it. Do not allow your old 'unworthy' feelings to rise up and rob you of the opportunity to reconnect with people who were at least concerned enough to phone you a few months ago.

If you have been unable to face the world for months, you may need to keep the visit short, maybe only an hour or so, but at least it's a start. If you do not have a car, you may want to book a taxi for the return trip home, then at least you will know in advance how long your visit will last.

If you are unsure that you will have anything to talk about, take along a recent photograph of a place you've been to, or take along a library book about the new destination or project you're planning to visit, whenever. Ask if they have ever seen the place, or if they know anything about it.

If they offer any kind of hospitality, be sure to accept. This signals that you are now ready to renew your relationship and you do want to be welcomed back into their world. Before you leave, invite them back to your place next week.

What if you do not have many relatives living nearby or friends are hard to find? If your relatives live in another part of the country, you may have to be content with a weekly phone call, until you are well enough to plan a visit.

If your friends are no longer interested in you, perhaps because you stopped returning their calls six months ago and if your apology has not allowed you to reconnect with them, you may just have to accept this and attempt to make new friends.

They do say that 'the best way to find a friend is to **be** a friend', so aim to make friends by being a friend to everyone you meet. You had friends once, so it is certain with the right set of circumstances you can make friends again!

If you take your children to school, talk to the other parents who are waiting at the school gates. Offer your services to help run the cake stall at the next school fundraising event – you will certainly be able to chat to others who are helping. If your confidence is at zero, say something like 'cake making is not really my thing, but I would certainly be willing to come and help erect the stalls or wash up and clear away afterwards'.

Invite their parents for coffee, the next time your child's friends are invited round. Or ask your social services or council of voluntary workers, if there is an older person in your neighbourhood, who might like an occasional visit. Join a rambling club or ask your local tourist board if there are any organised walks in your area. Take up a new hobby or interest, join a dance class or learn a new skill.

If you are interested in art, you could spend an afternoon looking around an art gallery, but this would be another day spent alone. Far better to find out if there is a water colour painting class for beginners in your area, phone the person in charge and pluck up all your courage to join in. Next time you want to visit an art gallery, you might just have made a new friend to go along with.

We looked in an earlier chapter at the possibility of you talking to your Church minister about your depression and asking him or her to help. Whilst making the point that this was not the time to 'jump ship' if you are facing overwhelming depression, what do you do in the future, if your vicar was less than helpful?

If your Church minister is one of those who is afraid to visit depressed people, fearing that he might 'catch it', there is not a lot you can do to change his attitude. If your Church minister says to you on a Sunday morning 'remember we are here for you' but cannot actually be bothered to visit you and make real that statement, will you have any confidence that he will be there for you in any other of life's events, such as bereavement?

If you are someone for whom your Christian faith is important and you have already been attending an established group of believers – do keep up your involvement with them, but if you have found that there has been little support for you in your present Church, you might want to consider whether there are other good local Churches around who would make you feel welcome.

Look in your phone book or at the library and consider going along. Do not necessarily look for something new or 'off the wall' – remember you are still fairly fragile and you could be vulnerable if you are thinking of getting involved with some kind of cult organisation, rather than an older established Church network. Just because some famous pop star wants to wear a red braid, or sit under a pyramid for hours at a time, does not necessarily mean they are living life in the best way.

If you have never been to a Church where people are friendly, welcoming and supportive, we suggest that you find a Church which runs an Alpha Course.

Alpha* is a nationwide initiative, which has been run by over 14,000 churches in the UK, as well as many thousands more in other countries. It involves people from all walks of life and the idea is that the course is aimed at absolute beginners. Do not think that everyone there will know all the answers and you will feel the 'odd one out' – even if you have never set foot in the building before – you will be made to feel welcome.

In fact, each evening starts with a free meal, then after a short talk or video, you will get to know more about the other members of your small group as you get involved in an informal discussion. This is your opportunity to ask any questions as you explore more about the Christian faith in a relaxed and 'laid back' way.

Do not worry that you will be 'made to go every week' which can be worrying if this was your only experience of Church when you were a small child. In fact, if you go to the first get-together and simply decide this is not for you, no-one will chase after you, putting pressure on you to attend another one.

If you decide that Alpha is not for you, there will still be other Churches in your area you could visit until you find a Christian family where you feel you belong. If you are serious about getting involved in a new Church, after your first visit, reflect on the following points:

- Were you made to feel welcome when you arrived?
- Did anyone speak to you, either before or after the service?
- Did this Church give the impression that newcomers were important, or did it feel more like a 'closed shop' with everyone chatting only to their friends?
- If you got to meet the Minister - Is he someone you could talk to?
- Was the worship enthusiastic? Could you read the words of the songs being sung?
- When the leader spoke, did you get the impression that the Bible is God's Word and that he believes it? Through the preaching of the Word, did you see the relevance in your day to day life?
- Did you get the overall impression that this Church believes in the power of prayer? Do you see yourself being able, at some future point, if not today, to ask someone there to pray for you?
- Does this Church have mid-week house groups or Bible Study where you could get involved with a smaller group of believers on a more informal basis?

If your visit was a positive experience, visit again and see how you feel, before you prayerfully make your decision about moving.

If this particular Church was not suitable for you, do not despair - try and find another one which is right for you. There is bound to be somewhere else that feels more like a family and where you could be welcomed into a new spiritual home.

If the idea of changing Church is unappealing, and you have few friends in your area, how will you approach the whole idea of getting on with your life, getting out there and meeting new people and hopefully making new friends?

What if your depression began after the sudden death of someone close to you? Those who have experienced the loss of a loved one through bereavement are sometimes surprised that they have still not 'got over it' even a year after the funeral has taken place. If you think you are still struggling with feelings of grief, we suggest that you contact Cruse* bereavement counselling.

If your depression was triggered by the death of a partner or a marriage breakdown, you may well be embarrassed or feel like an alien now you have to face life alone. If all your friends only knew you as part of a couple and now the invitations to dinner have all but evaporated, how will you resume a social life?

If you can just get through the coming months, however long it takes for you to feel more positive, you could reach a time when you decide you would like to meet someone new. Where do you start? If the suggestions we have already explored do not also bring you into contact with potential dates, you will have to cast your net a bit wider.

Ladies have sometimes questioned whether it would be safe to meet someone via an internet site or chat room. Whilst there have been successful relationships established via the internet, we would not recommend this approach - those very few members of society who have something to hide would usually prefer the anonymous idea of contacting a lady by email.

The last thing you need, just as your fragile confidence is starting to return, is to meet a man who, in his first email, pretended to be 31, but when you get to meet him, it is obvious that he is twice that age (or worse!)

What if you would really like to meet someone new, but your Christian (usually married) friends all say – 'if God wants you to have someone – He will send them along to you, to do anything about it just shows a lack of faith'. You could ask them what they do if God tells them to sell their house for instance. Do they sit at home, simply praying that God will send a buyer down their path, or do they take the practical step of putting their house on the market with the best estate agent in their area?

Most Christians do not count this last option as showing a lack of faith, but we assume that they will also be praying for a buyer, as well as making sure that their house is clean and tidy for every viewing!

If you want to meet someone new, for possible friendship and if you feel comfortable with the idea, you could try a Christian dating or Introduction agency*, listed in the UK Christian handbook (your Church minister or Library should have a copy).

Beware of using an agency from the phone book or online search engine, which looks like a Christian Agency, but is in reality a commercial agency, only listing 'Christian' as a group of people they want to help (along with Sikh, Muslim, Mormons and Jehovah's Witnesses.) Does the agency understand the differences, or are their clients all matched, simply because they are interested in 'religion'?

If you are now considering joining an agency, are you able to speak to anyone in charge by phone, or is it merely run like an internet site - usually only an electronic or printed list of names for you to contact?

If you have chosen what you consider to be an established, well organised agency and if you are able to speak to someone there, when you phone, try to speak to the owner and ask the following questions:

- How long has the agency been established?
- How successful has the agency been?
- Do they think they will be able to help you?
- What will they promise if they are unable to fulfil their obligations?

If, when you phone the first agency, you are never able to speak to someone in authority, no matter when you phone, then move on to the next agency listed. If, when you do get through to someone, they seem unable to answer your questions convincingly, phone another agency, maybe in another part of the country.

Suppose you do get through to your selected agency – before you decide to join, as well as asking all the above questions, ask if they have any advice for you to follow, in order to be more successful. For instance, if you are a lady 5 feet 10 inches tall, whilst you might want to only meet men living on your doorstep, I would suggest that you be willing to talk to possible introductions, wherever they live.

You might not have considered that more than half of all men who join any introduction agency do so because they are of less than average height. 'Average height' for a man is around 5 feet 7 inches tall.

Even if every superhero film you ever saw, casts the leading man as a 6 foot tall bodybuilder, the reality is that these men do not often need to join a dating agency! Be willing to talk to men who are shorter than your ideal, but living not too far away, or consider talking to any taller men who live further away than you had previously considered.

Similarly, if you are a man who is only 5 feet 3 inches tall and you have been faced with only much taller ladies in your day to day life, you may now have to take on board the fact that your ideal lady who is only 4 feet 9 inches tall might be living a hundred miles away but, if you **do** get to meet her and eventually **do** get to marry her, you will not be disappointed that she did not come from the same town, will you?

Above all, ladies please take the following advice on board:

Be realistic in your expectations about meeting someone around your own age. Yes, we know your **ex** husband was 10 years younger than you, but remember he is your ex husband – if you were able to flag up this relationship as being hugely successful, you might not now be wanting to meet someone new. If, when you were 30, you were fortunate enough to marry a man who was only 22 years old, do not assume that, now you are 68, you will be able to meet a man who is 58. Women outnumber men in the 55 plus age group and the men are aware of this too!

There again, if you insist on only meeting widowed men, you might find there are less of them than you had envisaged, for the following reason: in small villages most ladies in the local Church or community know that their neighbour's wife has died recently. It is not too long before some kindly widowed or divorced lady is beating a path to his door, bringing a cake she has just baked, or offering to do his ironing, or even help with child care, if that is a problem for a younger, widowed Dad.

What started out as a supportive friendship can sometimes turn out into a developing relationship, even if that was the last thing on his mind at the time.

Men, if your best buddy told you that he met his (much younger) girlfriend through 'Russian Mail Order Brides' – will he also tell you if she allows him to pay for her air fare on the pretext of going back home to get a visa and wedding outfit, never to return?

If a 76 year old man meets and marries a 26 year old girl from an overseas country, it may have little do to with his 'boyish' good looks or his 'witty conversation' but rather more to do with the promise of a visa, his healthy bank book and the imminent (she hopes) reading of his will! Yes, we know that **your** relationship is different, but be aware that she may not tell you all of her goals on the first or even the twentieth date!

Take your time in establishing a new relationship. If the person you have met recently is rushing ahead, talking about marriage after just two dates, why are they in such a hurry? A promising relationship will not become 'wrong' just because you took your time getting to know this person, will it? If they are right for you, then you will have the rest of your lives together and it is worth investing your time at this stage.

When establishing new friendships, trust your own instincts. If you have been dating for around three months and your new boyfriend never wants you to meet any of his family or friends and if he never allows you to meet him from work or go to his Church, that should set 'alarm bells' ringing. What is he trying to hide? Could he be already married or involved in another secret relationship?

Finally, having taken all of the sensible precautions, such as meeting in a public place, taking a mobile phone and getting a friend to phone you after the first hour of a date, to ensure that you are okay, relax and enjoy getting to know someone new, who might just turn out to be a good friend, or even better, a future partner.

As you set out to expand your social circle, after a time of actually being or simply feeling 'all alone', you may not be as confident as you would like to feel. You may need some help to face your worst fears.

Just about the time that you are considering getting back into social situations, whether that could be reconnecting with old friends or discovering ways of making new ones, your old fears might begin to rise to the surface, making it seem impossible for you to even step outside of your own front door, never mind appear inside a new public building or meeting place.

Write down a list of all your fears, and what you could do to minimise them. For instance, if you are a man who would like to learn ballroom dancing, your fear might be that you will appear unsuitably dressed ('all the men might be wearing white shirts and ties and I will feel out of place'). Rather than give this as an excuse for not trying something new, do your research, phone the organiser and find out what the dress code will be.

Another fear might be that you will be sat on your own all

evening and that no-one will talk to you. Again, when you phone the organiser, ask whether everyone will be with partners or whether you can come alone. Ask if you should only come if you can come as a couple. If this dance class wants to encourage new members, they will need to have a way of making new people feel welcome on a first visit, or no-one would ever return a second time.

So now you have made a list of your fears, done your research to minimise them and have been brave enough to try something new. After the event, re-visit your list of fears and write down what **actually** happened. Were all the other men wearing white shirts and ties? Were you the odd one out? Did you sit alone all evening? Did anyone make the effort to speak to you?

Hopefully, as you write down what actually happened on the night, you will have discovered that most of the fears you had, most of the things you spent time worrying about **never actually happened**. This should encourage you to face the truth that many of the fears that have prevented you joining in social occasions previously, are usually groundless in reality.

If, unfortunately, you were not made to feel welcome at this particular dance class, do not let this put you off learning to dance! Do not assume it was all your fault and retreat back to bed. Instead try another dance class, maybe in another town.

Use this approach of overcoming your worst fears in your everyday life. The more you are able to apply this principle, the more you will be able to break out of your destructive thought patterns.

We have looked previously at the way in which people who have low self-esteem or are depressed can talk about themselves in a negative, derogatory fashion: saying things such as 'I can never do anything right' or 'I am hopeless'. This will do nothing to lift your mood and will merely serve to drag you down further. Spending time celebrating your achievements and rewarding yourself for every positive outcome will remind you that there **are** things you can do.

If watching the language you use about yourself is important, then **all** your conversations with other people are of equal importance. There is a tendency for those who are depressed to be so preoccupied with themselves, that every conversation has to be turned around, back to them and how they are feeling.

If a friend tells you that she is feeling ill, do not reply 'you can't be feeling as bad as I do!' Whilst it is inevitable that your depression is dominating how you feel at the moment, those people who are trying to reach out to you in friendship do not want their feelings to be totally eclipsed by yours all of the time. Friendship is partly about listening to other people as well as talking about how **you** feel, what **you** have done, where **you** have been.

When you have been speaking about yourself, or your illness for a couple of sentences, get into the habit of saying to your friends 'that's enough about me – tell me what you have been doing'. As you make an effort to re-balance your conversations, ensuring that you are not only talking about yourself and how you feel, other people will at last get the impression that you are interested in them. Learn to ask questions which do not have 'Yes and No' answers.

For example, if you ask a friend, 'Did you have a good holiday?' They will usually reply 'Yes, thanks' or 'No, it rained every day!' If, instead you say 'tell me about your holiday' they will usually take a few minutes to talk about the place they have visited, the hotel they booked into and the highlight of their visit.

The other factor we all should remember is that we need to show the people close to us that we are thankful to them. When we are ill, it can be difficult to concentrate on anything other than our illness and how we feel, but just take a few moments to think 'when was the last time I said thank you to anyone?'

Perhaps you could plan (and it may happen in a few weeks time, rather than this week) to take someone out for a meal, if they have been 'there for you' during the days of your illness. If going out is not really something you could face, how about buying a small gift or a bunch of flowers? It is not really about the price of the gift, but more about the fact that you are now beginning to show your appreciation. If your finances are at zero, (or even worse!) you could just send a card, saying 'thanks for all you have done and are doing to help me'.

If you are now coming round to the idea of making sure other people know that they are important to you, this will have been a valuable lesson you have learned, especially as you try and establish new friendships.

GOAL

To re-connect with relatives and friends

To discover a new hobby or interest

To get involved in something in your community

To be proactive about making new friends

To find your way back to a place of faith or

To explore a new Church or Alpha group for the first time

To read Proverbs Chapter 26 verses 6 & 10 – thinking about true friendship and whether you have neglected your friends

CHAPTER 7 AN OSTRICH OR AN EAGLE?

Whilst you may long to soar like an eagle, the reality of your life might be that you act like an ostrich in most of your day to day living. If you were to ask the average man in the street what he knows about ostriches, most people would say 'they stick their head in the sand.' Now an ostrich keeper would tell you that there are many other attributes that ostriches share, but we mostly know them for only this one thing!

Maybe the people around you only know you as someone who 'puts his head in the sand' figuratively whenever you are in any danger or whenever you are facing some unexpected problem.

We have considered in the last chapter that it is only when we face our fears and overcome them, that we ever make any real progress in relationships. Now we are going to look at some of those other life scenarios which you might need to face up to.

In your daily life, whenever you face a challenge, what is the outcome? If your children ask you to attend their school concert, do you say 'ask me nearer the time'? You do not want to turn them down, but neither have you enough courage to attend or even to make a decision about attending.

Do you leave most decisions to other people, maybe your marriage partner, so that they carry most of the burden for you? Marriage is supposed to be a partnership, open to ideas and development from both of you, not left up to one overwhelmed and overworked person.

If you need to make a decision, do you put off thinking about it for as long as possible, then, at the last minute, decide quickly, without much consideration, before launching into a course of action?

Has this approach been less than successful for you? Have these hasty, ill-considered decisions led you to walk out of work? Or buy the wrong house? Or even start a new job, in the wrong organisation or the wrong part of the country? Do you hesitate, because you are unsure of any possible outcome?

Faced with decision making, this is another area you could now apply your new way of thinking. The Bible talks in James Chapter 1 verse 7 about a double minded man being unable to receive God's best – it actually describes him as 'unstable in all he does.' As we look together at better ways of decision making, aim to adopt these new ideas in your daily life, until they become second nature to you.

Making the wrong decision can sometimes start further back in the chain of events. For instance, the man who decides to quit work on an impulse because 'it all got too much for me' could later regret his hasty decision to walk out on his firm.

If he could only look into the future, he might well see himself as a broken man, who now feels a failure, with very little money in his pocket and without a good reference from his boss, to help him secure his next job. Having considered all the possibilities, would he have been so quick to walk out, if he had known that he would then find himself facing a year of unemployment?

A better course of action, which he avoided some weeks earlier, would have been to arrange an informal interview with his Manager, Supervisor or Human Resources Officer. At this interview he could have explained that, since the workload had increased because of staff shortages, he was no longer enjoying the job. Together they could have looked at all the issues involved and possible solutions to return him to a situation he could now manage.

If you are a Christian, involving God in your decision making is a vital part of your daily life. If you have never given this any thought, you need to realise that God wants to be in the driving seat of your life - do not relegate Him to the role of passenger. If you truly believe that He is the Creator, Almighty God, why would you want to make any moves without His loving guidance?

Proverbs Chapter 3 verse 5, talks about trusting the Lord, rather than leaning on your own understanding and when you begin to acknowledge Him, He will make your paths straight.

What does this mean, in practice? It means having God's view of things – His perspective on your life and work situation and His solution to any problem that comes along. Armed with His wisdom and good principles, you can have faith in your future decisions.

Next time you have to make a decision, try to adopt the following structured approach:

- Look at the whole situation you are facing, in a calm, rational way and ask God to guide you as you consider where He wants you
- Give yourself time and space to consider all your options
- Ask advice from loved ones, family or close friends
- Spend time on researching ways of overcoming difficulties
- Trust yourself to make a good decision

Say you need to decide about accepting a new job you have recently been offered. Of course, it almost goes without saying that you already need to be praying about this. Then, sit down or take a walk, whichever feels right to you and think about the issues calmly.

If you arrive home at midnight, after a hectic day or when you are hungry and the baby has started crying, do not make any decisions **now** (unless they include what to eat, how to settle the baby and how soon can you get to bed) – save your important decisions for the following morning!

In the morning, write down the arguments **for** and **against** staying in your current job, as well as those in favour of the new job or otherwise. Do not make your decisions based on finance alone – look at all the benefits and drawbacks for each job, objectively.

If you are coming to the point of accepting the new job, you might want to ask any friends if they know of this Company, and especially how they treat their employees. If you find out that they are the kind of firm who make staff redundant on a regular basis, giving only ten minutes to clear their desk, before marching them to a waiting taxi, you might decide not to join them!

If the only reason you are looking for a new job is that your present firm is moving to new premises further away and you have no transport, look at all your options. Could you take driving lessons? Would the firm arrange transport for you for the first few months after the move? Could you put a note on the staff noticeboard, or place an advert in the local newspaper, asking to carshare?

If you have a peace about your next course of action, go ahead. Once you have made what you feel is a good decision, do not continually put yourself down, assuming you have made the wrong decision.

The more you deal with issues of judgement, the easier your decision making will become and this will help you to become more confident in the future. Next time you are deciding about something as simple as booking a holiday, use this approach to arrive at your decision. Do your research, look at the resort you have in mind, read the reviews on the internet on your chosen hotel, talk to the travel operator about this area and then book. Learn to relax and trust your judgement.

If you have been made redundant and no job offer appears to be forthcoming, you may even be considering starting your own business. Do not immediately assume you will not be able to accomplish this. Do your research, consult the Government Business Development division in your area as well as the Business Manager at your bank. Write a realistic business plan.

Ask yourself the difficult questions – Do I have a sound business idea? Do I have any skills in this area, or do I know people who have the necessary skills to help me? How will I finance this idea, until it becomes profitable? What impact will this business have on my family life? Does my partner think this is a good idea and will she support me in this new endeavour?

If you have never learned to make considered, rational decisions, ask yourself whether you are a creature of habit, stuck in a rut. They do say that a rut is just a grave that is open at both ends!

Do you always go to the same familiar places, because this is where you feel secure? Are you afraid of trying anything new? If, until this point, you have always lived within your 'comfort zone', settling for a safe, predictable journey through life, you might want to think about how fulfilling this approach has been for you.

Instead of running away from making decisions, you might be surprised at how much you can achieve now that you have begun to make good decisions, based on sound judgement.

When you are in a difficult situation, how have you always dealt with it in the past? Do you escape through alcohol? A chance to wind down at the end of the day can quickly turn into 'I can't get to sleep at night, without a drink, it's the only thing that helps me to relax'.

Do you only cope if at the end of the day you can 'forget everything' by drinking large amounts of alcohol? It can seem easier to forget about how bad your day has been, rather than to deal with the difficulties that have made your day turn out bad. If you need two drinks every night this week to 'help you relax' or even to 'forget about everything', how many drinks will you need next month to get the same effect?

No one ever got into serious alcohol addiction by waking one morning and saying 'today I think I'll become an alcoholic'. It all started with just one glass and the wrong set of circumstances. If you need several glasses of wine every evening or a couple of large whiskies when you get home from the office each day, then your regular drinking pattern could be bringing on a whole new set of problems.

You may think that you are able to handle the amount you are drinking, but ask your family and friends how you behave when you have had a drink or two. Invite them to be honest about your pattern of drinking. If they say that you become argumentative after drinking, or if you are just the opposite and always become morose, inward-looking and sad after drinking, then you need to get help to change this aspect of your life and behaviour, before it destroys the relationships you most value.

Whilst it is true that most people are able to keep the small amount they drink under control, there are many others who are dishonest with themselves or their relatives about the amount they drink. If you hide the empty bottle underneath the rest of the rubbish in the bin or conceal the amount you are drinking in other ways, you should realise that heavy drinking nearly always leads to great loss.

It starts with loss of self-esteem and can lead to loss of promotion opportunities, because of poor time-keeping or poor judgement and may eventually lead to loss of a job.

Your drinking pattern this year which leads you to loss of self-control, causing arguments when you eventually arrive home, may next year have escalated to bring the loss of your marriage and family. This seems to me to be too high a price to pay!

Those who drink and drive might think they have it all under control until the day they run over someone else's child who later dies in hospital. If only they could turn back the clock. Those who have lived in a family where someone has been a heavy drinker would have a different point of view from those who think their drinking is never a problem.

They might tell you of the nights they have sat up, waiting for a loved one to come home, or of the nights they lay in bed, just waiting for the arguments to start. They might tell you of the night the police came, either to arrest their partner, after a hit and run accident, or even to break the sad news of a partner's suicide, caused by problem drinking.

If today your relatives or friends or work colleagues have been honest enough to tell you that your drinking habits concern them, you owe it to yourself to get the help you need, to overcome your destructive pattern of drinking, before it destroys you.

In the past, have you chosen to escape the unpleasant reality of your life through drugs? Young people can sometimes try so called soft drugs, simply because everyone else in their class has tried them.

Do not fall for the lie that cannabis is not addictive. Many of the people who now have clinical depression or other very serious mental health issues developed these problems after experimenting with cannabis. Having had normal behaviour all through their lives, even excelling in school work and gaining impressive exam results, there are some young people who then went on to be hospitalised for years, after experimenting with 'harmless' cannabis.

Then again, if you ask those people who are now addicted to non prescriptive drugs such as heroin or cocaine, what was the first drug they tried, many of them will have started on cannabis. This then became the doorway to those other drugs, which have ruined their lives. Like any other addiction, the people who started with so called 'soft' drugs and moved on to other things, always thought that they could 'handle it'- that they would never become an addict.

If you were to approach many of the organisations who run rehabilitation programmes for those with drug addictions, and asked them how many spare places they have on their courses, you might be surprised to find that most organisations have a waiting list. There are more drug addicts out there than there are places to help them come off drugs. The truth is that all of these drug addicts once thought they could 'handle it' – they never planned to become addicted.

Whether you are just at the stage of experimenting with cannabis or are now involved with other drugs as a way of coping with the pain in your life, consider getting help to overcome your dependence on drugs, before you lose your job, health or family.

Another area that can have a negative effect on lives and relationships is pornography. Before you turn the page, thinking this is not a problem for you, consider that most members of the population are constantly bombarded with images that are less than helpful.

As we have already considered previously, in advertising on television and in magazines, sex is used to sell everything from cars to perfume. It does not take a huge leap in imagination from accepting this as 'normal' to taking a peek at internet sites which ten years ago you might have considered to be outrageous.

Sexual temptation is not a new thing – the Old Testament

describes instances where a secret relationship has led to removal of the anointing of God over a man's life. These days we have seen examples of the resulting humiliation or loss of Christian ministry for those who have been unable or unwilling to overcome this subtle temptation.

From the headmaster or Church leader who acts upon his temptation to get involved with a teenage girl who has a 'crush' on him, to the Postmaster who eventually gets involved in fraud to give his young employee everything she needs to 'buy her silence' - all would later come to regret their moment of madness when viewed from the inside of a prison cell.

We need to understand that no-one usually sets out with the goal of destroying his marriage. Most likely the scenario starts with a friendship that gets too close, conveniently at a time when the husband is working away, or when the wife is too preoccupied, looking after small children, to consider paying the husband much attention.

That this could ever happen to anyone else, means that the unthinkable could even happen to you! All of the good done by all of the faithful Christians in your Church or town can be quickly undone by one moment of foolishness which could make newspaper headlines, even though you were sure that your secret was safe.

If you are ever tempted in this way, take steps to guard your marriage by guarding your thought life and looking afresh at the opportunities that just 'happen' to pop up in your daily life.

There are now even more options when it comes to gambling than there have ever been. While many people consider the lottery to be a harmless occasional flutter, other new methods of gambling are starting to emerge. Though there are too many dangers to list here, the main problem with these new ways, such as internet gambling, is the very fact that the gambling is hidden, concealed from family and loved ones.

Perhaps the secrecy of it all, adds to the excitement, or perhaps you delude yourself that, it cannot be wrong if no-one ever finds out about your gambling. It has been suggested that workers are losing more than £2 billion by gambling online whilst at work. It might surprise you to realise that many men, and even some women, have admitted that they have tried to gamble their way out of financial trouble.

Ask yourself whether, faced with your perceived lack of success in your work life, do you turn to online gambling or instead to the instant buzz of a slot machine, experiencing a high whenever you hear the clatter of coins as the machine pays out?

If gambling has become an issue (even if it is a secret issue) for you, would you not be better contacting Gamblers Anonymous* before it takes root in your life? If this destructive pattern of behaviour is not addressed, you could soon find yourself facing financial problems.

Whether your financial problems have been caused by a gambling habit, by over-spending or redundancy, this is a problem which will never go away on its own. Like your health issues, this situation will not get better if you simply choose to ignore it.

If you are only £100 overdrawn in your bank account today and you ignore it, by the time the bank have written to you (charging you around £20 or more, just to send you a letter) your debt will have risen. By the time your monthly mortgage direct debit has remained unpaid because of lack of funds, signalling a further letter from the mortgage company, along with their charges, you could have almost doubled your debt overnight.

Far better to write yourself a budget and stick to it. Make a list of all your income – do not have false expectations, only count your guaranteed monthly salary, not your anticipated production bonus which may or may not be added when the time comes.

Then write down all your outgoings, including how much you actually spend each week on socialising, clothes shopping and take-away meals. If you want to have an impact on your debts, there are only two ways of doing this – you either need to reduce your expenses or increase your earnings. Now, increasing your earnings might take a considerable time, involving sitting for another exam or arranging interviews for another job, not to mention actually securing the new job.

You would be better in the short term to control the only thing which you can do quickly, which is to reduce your monthly spending. If you have a serious overspending problem, look at everything – do not count any aspect of your outgoings as 'off limits'. Can you cancel the Cable TV subscription or your monthly internet broadband connection charge?

Instead of spending £20 socialising with friends every Friday night, could you arrange a 'girls night' in where a friend brings a DVD to watch, along with a bottle of supermarket wine to share? If you refuse to order a take away for the next month or so, you might have saved yourself around £40 toward your mortgage.

If your weekly look around the high street shopping mall always tempts you to splash out on the latest fashion, then find something else to do with your time! If you arrange to visit a relative instead, you might not only avoid the temptation of buying another item for your bulging wardrobe, you might also be given an invitation to stay for (free) lunch.

If, in spite of all your efforts to reduce your spending, you are still overwhelmed by the size of your debt, do not panic. You should definitely not be tempted to approach one of those firms advertising on the television, who promise to take all your debts and roll them into one 'easy', affordable, monthly payment. This may seem to be the answer to all of your prayers, but in reality will eventually increase your debt, spread your (initially smaller) payments over many more months or even years and make a handsome profit for the firm involved.

Most Citizens Advice Bureaux may have their own debt counsellor who would see you without making a charge and may also be a valuable source of free legal advice.

If your debts are really unmanageable, they may even write to all those firms who are sending you reminder letters and arrange to restructure your payments at no extra charge to yourself.

Finally if, in spite of addressing all the issues in your life over many months, your depression still has not lifted, you may need to look at other events in your past. Have you ever been under a 'generational curse?' As you discover more about your family history, have there been those in past generations who have committed suicide? Perhaps a misguided member of your family even voiced their foolish opinion that 'you would be better off dead!' Whilst the issue of being 'under a curse' does not apply to every Christian who is struggling with depression, if this has struck a chord with you, or if you have been involved with any area of occult practice, before becoming a Christian, you may need to look again at this area.

Arrange to talk these things through with a Christian leader who has experience of dealing with spiritual issues, and also has the faith to pray for you to be delivered in this area. Otherwise, contact a respected counselling organisation, such as the Acorn Christian Foundation* and ask for their help.

GOAL

To discover a new way of decision making

To be proactive about asking God for his wisdom when next making a decision

To explore and consider all possible outcomes

To have faith to move forward with your decision

To seek out the best available help if you have destructive habits or addictive behaviour

To explore creative ways of reducing expenditure rather than avoiding the issue

To read again James Chapter 1 verses 5 - 8

CHAPTER 8 WHO CARES ABOUT THE CARERS?

(Helping the friends and family of the depressed)

Whilst the whole focus of this book has been, quite rightly, on helping those who are depressed to take steps out of their darkness, behind every person facing such despair, there are usually family and friends, wondering what to do. How can you as their friend help them?

If you are a friend of someone who is depressed, you might be keen to help, but may be afraid that you will do or say the wrong thing. Do not let this fear prevent you staying in touch with your friend. He might have depression, but it is not catching! He or she will probably not contact you – most days just getting out of bed will seem like a huge assignment. They may even say that they want to be alone, that they can't face people. However, in spite of what they say, being left alone all day, week after week, will not help them in the long term.

They need the kind of friend who will resist the urge to say 'pull yourself together' and who will go out of his or her way to stay in touch, regardless of the fact that you will see little reward for all your time. Even if your friend does not appreciate the efforts you are making for them, at this moment in time, their family certainly will value your help and support.

In spite of the fact that your depressed friend never phones you back, do keep visiting them, even if you only stay for half an hour or so.

Do not phone first to ask if you can call to see them – if they are having difficulty facing people, they will never feel that today or even tomorrow is the right time – just call round to see them anyway. On the rare occasion that someone else has arrived at the same time, be prepared to only stay a few minutes and revisit later.

Having a regular visit from a friend, even if she only stays for a short while, will help overcome the feeling that they have been abandoned by 'normal' people or that their situation is hopeless and they will never get better. During your visit, talk about the things that are happening in your daily life or offer to play a board game.

If the weather is good, you could ask if they feel like having a gentle stroll or a drive in the countryside. You could also ask their partner or carer if there is anything you could do to help the family in any way. If you arrange with the family that you will call again the same day next week, you may well find that your visit is positively welcomed – but only arrange this if you are careful to stick to the arrangement. If your depressed friend begins to look forward to a visit from you and you fail to turn up, they will feel even more negative about themselves.

Anything you can convey to them about the fact that they will not always feel ill and that you expect them to make a full recovery will be beneficial. You could even say that you expect them to be back at Church, or your house group, or the cricket club (or wherever you used to meet together) next season. This will all help to bring hope to your friend who right now is feeling hopeless.

If you are the husband or wife of someone struggling with long-term depression, unless your medical centre is exceptional, or you have small children deemed to be 'at risk', you will be mostly forgotten in all of this. You may have already endured many months of difficulty, with equal measures of despair and frustration, as your loved one's depression has made her (and perhaps also forced you to) withdraw from many aspects of life.

In order to help you survive and continue with your life and work, you should first of all accept that there is no quick fix solution to your partner's problems. Of course you want me to say that he or she will be better just as soon as they have read Chapters 1 to 7 of this book, but holding on to this fantasy will not make it happen.

Instead, assume that it will take about a year for them to become the person they used to be, before the depression took hold. If they get better more quickly, it will be a wonderful bonus. At the very least, this thinking will prevent you putting your own life 'on hold' - assuming that you will see how your loved one feels next week, before accepting the next invitation to a house-warming party or a night out with friends.

Their recovery will usually depend on any number of factors, largely outside of your control. Your loved one may, or may not, welcome your suggestions to help them cope with their situation. Accept that they have choices to make and however frustrating the whole situation may feel to you, expect that your main role will be that of supporter. Offer endless amounts of encouragement and regular prayer (even if your loved one does not want to be involved in a regular prayer life with you).

Outside of your immediate family circle, be realistic about the fact that most people are sympathetic for about 6 weeks (or however long it takes for a broken leg to heal) if someone is ill. If the illness is something which is invisible to the vast majority of people, especially if no-one in their family has ever suffered from depression, they will have little concept of how you will be feeling.

Your loved one might have gone through a time when they did not want you tell anyone they were depressed and your friends would not then understand why you have declined every recent opportunity to go out and visit them. As a Christian, you will be aware that you have an enemy. The Devil will do all he can to make you feel despairing, isolated or stigmatised by your partner's condition.

You should remember that even the apostle Paul had times when he was greatly troubled. We read in the 2nd letter to the Corinthians Chapter 7 verse 5, words such as 'no rest'...'harassed... conflicts...fears within' – but then he reminds us that it is 'God who comforts the downcast' and in this instance at least, God's comfort came through for Paul by the appearance of a friend (Titus) who had himself first been comforted and prepared by God.

Once you have accepted that the situation will not improve overnight, phone, write or visit your closest friends or family. Explain the situation to them – using words like:

'Mary has been suffering from depression since February – she has only just been allocated a mental health worker, so it might take a while, but we as a family are counting on your support to get through this.'

Out of four friends or relatives who are now aware of the problem, expect maybe one or two to get alongside you and help. Even amongst caring Christians, there are many who have never experienced anything similar to the situation you are facing, preferring to think that 'this doesn't happen to us'. They may not be uncaring or unsympathetic – they may have very busy lives or just feel unqualified to help.

The truth is that you are probably not looking for answers from experts – you just need some extra support from those who care about you. If they could pitch in and help or possibly share a little of your burden, life would become more 'normal' for you and your family.

If you have small children and, especially if you are trying to hold down a job as well as keeping the family home ticking over, you will definitely need as much help as you can get. Ask relatives if they could help with organising a rota for meals, cleaning or collecting the children from school. If you only have a few elderly relatives, perhaps social services could arrange some extra help for you. Could your salary stretch to providing a paid cleaner for a few hours on a Friday, so that you would not have to spend all your weekend cleaning?

Make no mistake, if you are trying your best to cope with a partner who is suffering from long-term depression, you will need to ensure that you are not also in danger of 'going under', whether through an overwhelming work-load or simply because you rarely have the chance to get out and mix with other people.

If your partner has been depressed for some time, or is given to long bouts of anxiety, they may not want you to leave them alone, even for a few hours. At the beginning, you may want to be sympathetic, but after three or six months, it is simply not possible for you to be 'joined at the hip' twenty four hours a day. You need to have times when you can have some relaxation and continue with your hobbies or special interests.

Arrange with a relative or friend to come over to be with your partner, whilst you have a break. With even one friend 'on board' you should get out your diary and put some plans in place – a regular night out perhaps – an evening at the theatre or a visit into town to watch a music concert.

Do not wait until your partner has recovered from depression, before you pick up the threads of your life again. If you wait until your partner feels like suggesting you go out together, it may never happen. Depression is an 'all consuming' illness and the whole focus of attention for your partner will be on themselves. How **they** are feeling will dominate their waking moments – they will have no time left over and little energy left to consider how you are feeling about all of this.

If you are going to have any quality of life, **you** are going to have to be the one that arranges the events which make up a social life together. If you have a young family, they, as well as you, need some fun times together. Visit your nearest tourist information centre and pick up a handful of leaflets for attractions in your area. Let each of your children choose an event or activity for the whole family to get involved in over the next few weekends.

If your partner says she is too depressed to join in, even after all your encouragement, you may have to set off without her. Concentrate all your efforts on you and the rest of the family having a good time, rather than regretting the fact that your partner did not come and worrying about her being left behind. If that is her choice today, she may just choose to come next time, especially if the children come home with pictures of the places they visited or show enthusiasm about the animals they have seen.

Book a holiday or weekend away – you've earned it! If, as well as working, you have been running the home with very little help and caring for a family, recognise that, during this time, you have actually been carrying two or three work loads. If you do not have a break, either with or without your partner, you may well need medical help yourself and then where would your family or your partner be?

If you feel guilty about the idea and expense of a holiday, maybe you ought to check what it could have cost for a week's stay at a private clinic, if you had not been caring for your partner. You would probably be surprised to find the level of care you have been providing for nothing, would have cost hundreds of pounds just for one week, never mind the months you have been there supporting, encouraging, advising, not forgetting the cleaning and cooking!

If your children are grown up and you are now on your own as a couple, arrange to have regular weekends away. Look for special offer hotel breaks advertised in the weekend newspapers or on the internet or teletext. The change of scenery, as well as having your meals cooked, will be good for you.

If your partner protests that they will not enjoy it because they are depressed, explain that you will just be together as a couple – you don't expect them to be the 'life and soul of the party' for everyone else in the hotel – the weekend away is not a miracle cure for their condition, it is simply a chance to relax together.

Approaching a break in this way will take the pressure off you and them. You are entitled to have a change of routine and a chance to 'recharge your batteries' and they will hopefully understand that you do not expect them to come home 'cured' from their illness, or even saying they enjoyed it!

Out of season, you might be able to afford a special offer weekend at a hotel with leisure facilities. The chance to have some healthy exercise as you swim together in the hotel pool, will be an added bonus.

Do not be tempted to cancel your break away when your partner says 'but I'm depressed – I won't enjoy it'. After all, would they be any **less** depressed if you stayed at home instead of going away? Being realistic about their situation may mean that you have to settle for a weekend in the Lake District, rather than a helicopter ride over the Grand Canyon, but this is no reason why you should not plan some kind of break away together.

As well as making time for holidays together, look at your weekly routine and see if there are ways to make life more interesting. A regular Friday night or Saturday lunchtime drive out to the countryside, followed by a meal out might give you both something to look forward to.

We have already looked at putting suitable rewards in place for the depressed person who has finally been able to make some effort with the daily chores. Look again at these suggestions for yourself. If you are a lady, when did you last arrange to have your hair styled, or have a manicure or an aromatherapy massage? If your wife is the one who is depressed, you, as her caring husband, are quite entitled to watch your local football team or have a night out playing snooker with your friends from work.

If you have a parent who is suffering from depression, you may wonder how you can help them get better. There is a fine line (which you must not cross) between offering loving support to your mother or father and actually allowing them to look to you as their mother or father figure! If you are the child in such a family, you must allow yourself to be a child if you are to develop your own distinct and unique gifts and personality. You must avoid at all costs the temptation to become your parents' rescuer or problem solver. Parents or children for that matter can sometimes face depression because of poor choices they have made in the past and although it is a painful lesson to learn, rescuing them from the reality and outcome of those choices, will not help them make right choices in the future. For the sake of your own health and mental well-being you have to set boundaries for what help and support you are able to offer. For instance, it is unreasonable for your parent to expect you to abandon your own social life and friendships, simply to fill their empty spaces. If you think about the coming weekend, this is always going to be a difficult time for people who are depressed – your parents might have been taught to expect that the weekend will hold the promise of something exciting and a change from everyday routine. But it is not for you to organise their whole weekend, full of stimulating ideas, to make them feel better. Trust me, when you have bent over backwards to arrange something you hope they will enjoy, the response will usually be the same – 'it would have been alright if I had not felt depressed, but I didn't really enjoy it!' The end result will be that you have given up your weekend to entertain someone who refused to take pleasure in the entertainment offered to them with every good and kind intention.

It would have been more sensible for you to plan some times at the weekend for you to spend with your own friends and one part of the weekend (say one evening) with your depressed parent. I am giving you permission to go to that party, meal out or church youth group activity – you must not ever say to your friends 'I cannot come out with you because I cannot leave my sick mother or father'. With the support of friends in the Church and other family members, you must release your parent to God's care, especially allowing that to be channelled through others.

When you look at the balance of your life, ensure that you have times of fellowship with the Lord (remember He wants to be your friend, so spend time enjoying Him) especially times when you allow Him to encourage you from what you read in His Word. Look at how much time you spend allowing other people to support you and how much time you allocate to just having fun or recreation. Recreation is such a good word – it reminds us that the time we spend just walking, listening to good music, sitting in the garden or some other special place can become times when God can literally re-create our thoughts and shape our responses to difficult situations. As well as the day to day tasks we all have to undertake, whether we work or study, we need times when we can relax and unwind and times when we can invest in relationships that are special to us. You cannot choose what other people do with their time, you cannot choose how your parent responds in difficult circumstances, you can only choose how you respond. If your depressed parent can never be bothered to clean the house, do the washing or eat healthily, you cannot make them do these things. You can choose to eat healthily yourself (and maybe cook for them one of the days at the weekend) you can choose to do your own washing and take pride in your appearance. You can choose to clean your own bedroom and maybe move the furniture around, if a room makeover is outside of the budget at the moment. Declare in your heart that you will not become a victim, there are areas you can control and, by God's grace and strength working in you, you must refuse to be buried in a black hole, not of your making.

There are three threads which, if combined together, will help you keep a grip of things when faced with an overwhelmingly challenging home life - we have already looked at one element: having one or two supportive friends, relatives or colleagues, especially those who will have the imagination to pray with and for you, rather than just asking how you are. The second is ensuring that you are still involved in some kind of social life or Church family. But the most important focus for the child of God has to be in recognising that God is still in control (in spite of every 'evidence' which seems to show the opposite). He is working things out for you (however long it takes) and He is still worthy of your praise.

You might come to God feeling a huge sense of loss or disappointment – tell Him how you are feeling, you can be honest with Him. The Bible gives a wonderful picture of the prophet Habakkuk who came to God in great despair – 'no grapes on the vines...the olive crop failed...no cattle in the stalls' (I'm sure you get the drift) yet he was still able to rejoice in God (and he takes the personal line here) calling Him '**my** Saviour'.

However black things are for you, however hopeless things might be looking, it is true that God is still your Saviour – He will enable you to keep a grip in a difficult place (like a deer stands firm in a tight spot, living on the edge!) If not today, there **will** come a day when you will be able to stand in awe of God's deeds and praise Him for all He has done in your life.

GOAL

To read 2 Corinthians Chapter 7 verses 5 – 7

To recognise that you need help and support

To discover who God is sending to support you and allow them 'in' to encourage you

To explore all opportunities for you to have a social life & make future plans for relaxing days out or holidays together

To stay in regular contact with your friends, family and your Church family

To Read Habakkuk Chapter 3 verses 2 & 17 - 18

In faith, remind yourself again of that truth in verse 2, re-phrasing this: 'I will stand again in awe of your deeds'. Claim this as God's promise for you!

CHAPTER 9
HEALTHCARE PROFESSIONALS AND MINISTERS

As those who have a professional or spiritual interest in seeing people who are suffering from depression made whole again, what should your mandate be? What is certain is that your workload may be increasing on a daily basis, whilst you still have only the same 24 hour clock that you had last week. In looking at the ever increasing workload of those involved in certain aspects of mental healthcare, how can your time be used more effectively?

Firstly, do not assume that your depressed patient will get up at 8 am to make an appointment to fit in with **YOUR** system! Most depressed people would struggle to get out of bed at 10 am, never mind 8 o'clock. If you have an unrealistic expectation of arranging an appointment so early in the day, your patient may simply not turn up, which will be a waste of your valuable time and effort and another week lost in your patient's life. She may seriously wish to get better, in spite of being unable to make an effort to fit in with your timetable. Be radical enough to arrange an afternoon appointment and ensure that your patient is able to keep it.

Rather than arranging an appointment for your patient to come to you in your surgery, why not arrange to visit them at home? Yes, we know it will take more time, but if your patient gets better after only three months of this kind of care, you might have saved yourself nine months of future appointments and might also have avoided having to deal with the distressing aftermath of the 'one in seven' suicides, according to a recent report, affecting seriously mentally ill patients.

If you visit them at home, you would be able to see what kind of support they are getting and would have also discovered how the rest of the family are coping in this situation. You may be relying on their family support to get them to any future appointments on time. Also their loved ones may be looking to you for some kind of hope that their family situation can improve, given time and the right kind of help.

Ensure that your patient is seen by a suitably qualified professional. If you arrange for a depressed person to be seen for their initial assessment by a trainee, they might be devastated to learn, after an hour of 'pouring out their soul' that the person they shared confidential thoughts with, had moved on to their next assignment just a week later.

Whilst acknowledging that trainee mental health care assistants do need to be trained, this assessment interview should be conducted with another senior staff member present, who is going to continue looking after the patient, in an ongoing situation, without the need for the patient to keep going over old ground again.

It has always been acknowledged as best practice in Christian counselling, that a man needing help should be offered counselling with another man, rather than a woman. Whether within the NHS or private sectors, mental health care workers should also take on board the fact that a mature man would nearly always feel better talking to another man, rather than a much younger female, even if this may take a great deal of time and initiative to arrange.

If you are in Christian ministry as a Church minister or house group leader, God has entrusted these sheep to your care. Even if, (or especially when) these sheep are sick, God is counting on you to get involved. Can He trust you to be faithful in this less glamorous part of your ministry?

Maybe you have held back until now, either because you feel that long term depression is out of your area of expertise or because you are respecting the patient's right to involve you and ask for your help.

First of all, as we have already considered, accept that someone who is very depressed may not even be able to make the effort to get up in the mornings, never mind appear at your house to ask for your help. The initiative in this case will need to come from you. At the very least, if they are in a loving and caring Christian family, their relatives may be eternally grateful for your input, prayer and support.

Do not wait to be invited, the depressed person may have told their wife or husband that they did not want anyone to know about their depression. If you think their husband or wife will tell you at Church over coffee on Sunday morning that their partner is very depressed, you are probably expecting the impossible.

Instead, if you have heard 'confidentially' that there is a problem with clinical depression, go and visit them. If you take the time to appear at their home, they will probably welcome you and will be honest enough to tell you some of the difficulties they are facing.

If you fear that you do not have the resources to get involved, do your research and find the details of the best Christian counsellor in your area who might be able to help, either directly with the depressed person or their family. At the very least, you could assure them that you will be praying for them and that you will return next month (or whenever seems appropriate to you) to see how they are.

Take time to consider whether your Church provides any kind of ongoing support to people inside or outside the church, with mental health issues. Or, in your Church, are these people stigmatised even more? One thing you can be sure of, if one person or family in your congregation is facing these difficulties at this moment in time, there will be others in the future. These issues will not simply go away.

You may long in your heart for your Church to become known as a place where people commit their lives to Christ and where mature Christians grow and develop their ministry gifts. But, have you taken on board that the Church is also a hospital, filled with sick people, waiting to get better?

The true Church of Christ will be a mixture of both of these pictures – as new Christians become mature under your teaching ministry, hopefully they will begin to reach out with compassion and the love of Christ to their friends and neighbours, who may be even more fragile and hurt than you could ever know.

Whilst, naturally, you would wish to spend much of your time with those of your congregation who value and encourage you most, recognise that God has placed in you the gifts to ensure that these 'other sheep' in your care are equipped for worship and service.

If, at this moment in time, you feel that you are ill-equipped for this side of your ministry, remind yourself again that the same Spirit which raised Jesus from the dead is living in you! Ask the Holy Spirit to come and fill you on a daily basis with all the resources you need to fulfil His purposes.

In considering what your 'mission statement' should be, can you look at the one outlined by the Master? In Luke Chapter 4 verses 18 and 19, Jesus quite clearly reveals that God has plans to proclaim freedom for the prisoners and release for the oppressed. How are you fitting into His plans?

As you and the rest of your ministry team move forward in faith to become better equipped, arrange training for them. Cover all aspects, ranging from 'how to befriend the unlovable' to 'how to pray for the sick, expecting God to move'! Emphasise that your ministry to the depressed is to be a twofold approach – first of all to those who are depressed themselves and also to their families, who live daily carrying an extra burden. The book of Isaiah is a great place to start – Chapter 35 reminds us to say to those with fearful hearts 'be strong...do not fear...your God will come'.

Chapter 43 talks about a people who are valuable and precious to God. Whilst we might prefer to paint a picture of the Christian walk being one without any problems or setbacks, the truth of Scripture reveals that God is with us, even when we feel out of our depth – whether we walk through deep waters or through fires.

The promise of God quite simply is that, even if we feel overwhelmed, we will not drown – He has promised to be with us. As Christian ministers or just members of the local body of Christ, we commit ourselves to stand alongside each other and especially to walk with those who face an uphill battle on a daily basis.

GOAL

To read again Romans Chapter 8 verse 11, asking the Holy Spirit to fill you afresh each day

To remember that God has placed in you all the resources you need to fulfil His purposes

To ensure that the Church is a place to grow for all people

To read Luke Chapter 4 verses 18 & 19 and adopt this as your mission statement

To make plans to move forward with God into what may be unfamiliar territory

To arrange suitable training for your ministry team

To read again Isaiah Chapter 35 verses 3 & 4 and Chapter 43 verses 1 - 4

CHAPTER 10 FUTURE PROTECTION

Now that you are on the road to recovery and feeling much better, there are some things you need to put in place to ensure that the possibility of becoming depressed again in the future is minimised.

Recognise that you are always going to be vulnerable in this area. This is not a criticism of you, just a statement of fact. In everyday life, there are people who may be prone to asthma attacks and have to be careful whenever they have a chesty cold, recognising they are more vulnerable in this area.

So for you, your vulnerable area is that of depression and if you have discovered situations which, for you, are the triggers causing you to start on a downward spiral, you may help yourself to prevent future attacks.

Maybe for you there is a certain anniversary of the death of a loved one and you know that around this date every year you start feeling depressed, remembering all you shared and mourning the fact that your life has now changed for ever.

Instead of dreading the yearly date, heralded by placing a 'memorial' advert in a local newspaper, allow yourself to break with tradition, to do things differently. Plan ahead to do something uplifting on the date, take along a sympathetic friend who has already been instructed by you, not to allow you more than an hour talking about your loved one. Whilst you may never be the life and soul of the party on this particular date, if you can break the cycle of gloom and the temptation to spend the day alone, you may just prevent yourself starting down the familiar road of becoming depressed.

For many people Christmas can promise to be a time of great joy. They plan for this time of year as soon as the summer holidays are over. They spend weeks shopping and wrapping gifts, not to mention cooking mountains of mince pies. They anticipate spending the whole of December and early January welcoming friends and relatives in front of a roaring log fire.

By the beginning of February, when all the festivities are over, reality sets in and they realise that, not only are they physically exhausted and overstretched financially, but there is a whole ten months before they can do it all over again! This scenario could just be their trigger leading them on the downward spiral of depression.

So if this rings a bell for you, how could you do things differently this year? Perhaps you could make a note on your calendar that your Christmas planning only starts in October for a change. Then you could aim to discover the real meaning of Christmas. Surely it is about much more than shopping, presents and cooking? As a Christian, have you truly taken on board that 'Jesus is the reason for the season'? If you strip away all of the activities which do not really celebrate His coming, what are you left with?

Check whether your attitudes are really just a thinly disguised attempt to show off, as you buy the most lavish gifts, or even a subconscious desire for perfection, as you slave over a hot stove from morning till night to cook up a storm, worthy of 'Masterchef!'

As you examine your motives, perhaps you could begin by acknowledging that Christmas, wonderful though it is, only lasts for around a week. At its most basic, it is just one special day and all your cooking and gift wrapping will not change someone's life for ever. Also, if you don't buy your eldest son the same gift all his mates are getting from their parents, his life will not come to an end!

If you are having friends and family to stay, would they value the chance to share the cooking with you, or provide the sweet course? Could they plan to stay over one night, rather than the five nights they stayed for last time? Of course, it is more difficult if you have built up family traditions over many years, whereby the in-laws always come to stay for a week at Christmas, but it only takes one year to break the tradition and, if it causes you and the rest of your family such stress, maybe this should be the year you break with tradition.

When you do your Christmas shopping, plan to spend around half of what you spent last year. With the money you save, book a weekend break or short holiday in January or February, to re-enforce the message that life goes on all through the year and doesn't end after Christmas.

If finances are in short supply, do not be tempted to spend more than you can really afford. Forget the idea of overstretching yourself financially to provide that 'must have' gift for your child and then paying later next year. All the adverts on the television and the resultant 'pester power' from your children are aimed exactly at people like you!

Work out a budget that you can realistically stick to and don't overspend. The other thing you could consider is suggesting to extended family or friends that you have an 'inventive' Christmas – where you only spend a maximum of, say £3 on each person, but you have to buy something which reflects an interest of theirs.

Or, if you have a large family, meet up in October and draw each others names out of a hat, so that everyone only has to buy one present at Christmas, but every person is included.

Start positive family traditions, rather than those which simply realise the expectations of the toy industry. For example, it might seem cute to you as the mother of a three year old, to have them write a list of gifts they would like to have in their Christmas stocking. I promise it will not feel cute when they are ten or eleven years old and they have raised their expectations to order from you the latest playstation or new computer, which you could not afford, even if you thought it was a good idea.

Perhaps you would be far better to bring up your three - year old with the reminder that 'at Christmas, we always have surprises in our family'. This will release them from false expectations and will also release you from the anxiety surrounding your inability to pay for huge gifts that are outside of your budget.

If you are facing your first Christmas alone, after bereavement, or marriage breakdown, it can be extremely painful to watch everyone else having a good time, knowing that you have never felt less like celebrating. So, aim to do things differently this year. Do you have a close friend who is in a similar situation and could you plan to spend Christmas away from home?

If that is not a possibility, you could maybe plan to invite a friend over for a Christmas day meal. If you know that you will feel miserable, do not deny your sad feelings, allow time and space for them. Perhaps at midnight on Christmas Eve, you could light a candle, remembering the times you shared, but also making a commitment to move on in the grieving process, as you face the New Year.

You may think that we have spent a long time considering whether for some people, Christmas can be the trigger which leads them to depression. This has been done for a very good reason. If you ask the counselling organisations such as Relate* or the Samaritans* which time of the year increases their workload, they would agree that they take many more phone calls immediately after Christmas from those who are depressed or from those who face marriage breakdowns. Of course, some of those marriage breakdowns might have occurred because of foolish decisions made at the office Christmas party, by those whose wrong actions were encouraged, as a result of drinking too much.

On Christmas Day, you will usually see a group of Jehovah's Witnesses going door to door, so perhaps they are also more aware of the disillusionment felt by many people, faced with the wrong emphasis on Christmas. Unlike them, however, we are not suggesting that we no longer celebrate Christmas, only that we celebrate with great joy a Christmas with the right values.

So we make no apology for covering this topic in detail, hoping that this year will be a time for you to consider your motives, refuse to succumb to the pressure of the advertising industry, and discover the true meaning of Christmas.

But maybe for you, Christmas has never been anything other than a lovely time of celebration, stress free and full of enjoyment. Perhaps there are other things which cause you problems.

Because we are all different, there are some things which cause you to become depressed, which do not cause other people difficulties. Write down the following sentence: 'I always get depressed whenever...' As you complete the sentence, thinking about a scenario which is a personal trigger for you, you may discover how to help yourself in the future. For instance, you may have traditionally started being depressed every time you have faced lack of work.

We have covered this in depth in earlier Chapters, but for you personally it may be vital to put some strategies in place in the months before you know your job is coming to an end. You may need to share with your house group that you do not cope very well with the prospect of having to look for work.

Perhaps, as you share it with your close group of friends, not only will they offer to pray for you, but they might also be the very people who will hear about a job, before it has been advertised and be able to point you in the right direction, for securing an interview.

If for you, the depression has always happened whenever your partner has to work away from home, are there practical steps you could take, such as being free to go with him, if he has to travel to another country. Or if that is not practical, could you put arrangements in place to have a friend come and stay with you, while he is away?

Maybe you are one of those rare people who hate the thought of going away on holiday – you cannot cope with the upheaval of your daily routine and you miss your family and friends, making you miserable the whole time you are away.

Look at alternatives. Would your partner agree to going away in a group which included your family? Or if a week away really is too much for you to contemplate, could you instead have four or five long weekends away in this country, scattered throughout the year?

You may have gathered by now, that I do not share the opinion of some employers who make life as difficult as possible for their overworked employees to have a holiday. I happen to believe that people work much better all through the year if they know that they are going to be able to take a break, when they have booked their holidays in line with company policy and considered the needs of others.

At least, I do not believe that employees work any harder all through the year, if employers set out to make them miserable by not allowing them to take a holiday, without feeling guilty. Even just allowing staff to have a (previously booked) day off may make them more creative when they return to work.

If you, as their manager or employer, step in and do their job, whilst they are off, it may also make you more creative, as you come up with an idea to work more efficiently. At the very least, you may realise the downside of the job which makes your employee feel depressed and you may, in future work together with them, to change things!

Whatever your past pattern has been, if you are prone to any kind of depression, you need to make the effort to have regular sleep. Not for you the 'burning the candle at both ends' approach adopted by typical university students.

If you have trouble actually getting to sleep in the first place, make some practical adjustments to help yourself:

1. If your bed is old and lumpy, replace the mattress, or buy a 'mattress topper' to make it more comfortable.
2. Ensure the bedroom temperature is just right, neither too hot nor too cold. Open a window wide enough to allow fresh air.
3. Do your exercising early in the day, not late at night, as this over-stimulates the mind.
4. Have a warm bath, followed by a cup of milky hot chocolate
5. Sprinkle a few drops of lavender oil on your pillow and listen to some relaxing music.
6. Read a pleasant book (not a thriller or murder mystery!)

Finally, if you worry about problems or jobs you need to finish tomorrow, consider making a list, as described earlier in the book. You could even roll up the paper list and place it inside your shoes, left outside the bedroom door, reminding you that your anxieties are also best left outside the bedroom door and should not be tackled until the morning!

Suppose you have tackled all the information contained in this book, have faithfully kept your doctor's appointments, taken your medication as prescribed, but feel no better than you did on day one.

Have you truly made Jesus Lord of your life? We are not thinking about Church membership or even Church attendance here, but the conscious decision to commit your life to Christ, receive His forgiveness and healing and allow His Spirit to empower you every day. As you seek to live for Him and serve Him daily, He has promised to supply all the resources you need to live a victorious, fulfilling life.

In fact, someone has described the feeling as a 'God shaped emptiness', when people live each day without allowing Christ to be Lord of their lives. Whatever you do to feel better, you still experience 'dis-ease'. In other words you are ill at ease every day, following the wrong goals or simply trying to make it through on your own, in a way that you were never designed to live. You were created by the Creator God to live in harmony with Him, and without Him there is no peace – you will continue to look for what is missing in your life. If you have ever watched your children doing a jig-saw puzzle, things are going along fine until they get to the end and find there is a piece missing. They pick a piece that looks something like the space they have left. Though they may try their best, looking at the wrong piece from every angle, just 'wishing it right' will not make it fit the space it was never made for.

That, in essence, is the dilemma you may be facing if you have tried everything you know to live a fulfilling life, outside of Christ. However hard you try, you will still come back to the thought that 'there must be more to life than this!'

The truth **is** that there is more, **much** more and you can only experience God's best if you recognise His claim on your life and the fact that He has come that you should experience 'life and have it to the full' as described in John Chapter 10 verse 10. Jesus here describes Himself as the good shepherd who gave His life to care for the flock. If this has never been explained to you in a way that you can understand, or if it has never been presented to you in a way that you can respond, can we encourage you to make those enquiries and take those steps by contacting a local Christian Church minister in your area or by phoning the UCB prayer-line*.

In your search for peace and freedom from anxiety or depression, do not settle for anything less than the wholeness Jesus died to bring!

GOAL

*To read John Chapter 10 verses 7 - 11
and especially verse 10*

*Recognise your vulnerable areas
which trigger depression for you*

*Consider enrolling on an Alpha
course in your area*

*If you are feeling desperate phone
the UCB Prayer-line*

*Make time to get to know Jesus as the
Good Shepherd or to 'reconnect' with Him,
if your depression has made you feel unworthy*

Do not settle for less than the best!

LIST OF HELPS

AA
(Alcoholics Anonymous)
P.O. Box 1
Stonebow House
Stonebow
York YO1 7NJ
Tel: 01904 644026
www.alcoholics-anonymous.org.uk

Help those affected by alcohol addiction. Local Support Groups.

ACORN CHRISTIAN FOUNDATION
Whitehill Chase
High St Bordon
Hants GU35 0AP
Tel: 01420 478121
www.acornchristian.org

Organise Counselling Courses and Healing Ministry

ALPHA
(also Alpha Marriage Course)
The Alpha Office
Holy Trinity Brompton
Brompton Road
London SW7 1JA
Tel: 0207 581 8255
www.alphacourse.org

Run Alpha courses nationwide. An informal introduction to Christian belief.

Care Centres Network
Tel: 0800 028 2228
www.careconfidential.com

Pregnancy crisis and post abortion helpline.

Consumer Credit Counselling Service (CCCS)
Tel: 0800 138 1111

Help those with debt problems.

CRUSE – Bereavement Care
126 Sheen Road
Richmond
Surrey TW9 1UR
Tel: 0208 940 4818
Tel: 0870 167 1677

*Bereavement
counselling available
nationwide.*

FAIRTRADE Foundation
Room 204
16 Baldwin's Gardens
London EC1
Tel: 0207 405 5942
www.fairtrade.org.uk

*Help producers in
poorer countries get a
fair price for the goods
they produce.*

GAMBLERS ANONYMOUS
P.O. Box 88
London SW10 0EU
Tel: 0870 050 8880
www.gamblersanonymous.org.uk

*Help those affected
by gambling.*

LIFE – Save the Unborn Child
Tel: 01926 421 587
www.preghelp.org.uk
www.lifeuk.org

*Pregnancy
counselling.*

Mercy Ministries UK
Tel: 01535 642042
www.mercyministries.co.uk

*Ministry for women
16-28 with life
controlling disorders.*

NEW DAY INTRODUCTIONS
Tel: 01706 224049
www.marriageintroductions.co.uk

Marriage Introductions, covering the whole of the UK - established since 1989 - has 2 separate services:

1) General Service for Non-Christians

2) Exclusively Christian Service

NICHOLASTON HOUSE
Penmaen, Gower
Swansea SA3 2HL

Christian retreat, healing and conference centre, organise Overcoming Eating Disorders and other weekends.

Books by Helena Wilkinson
www.helenawilkinson.co.uk

Insight into Eating Disorders.

RELATE
Herbert Gray College
Little Church St
Rugby CV21 3AP
Tel: 0845 456 1310
www.relate.org.uk

Marriage Guidance.

S.A.D.A
P.O. Box 989
London SW7 2 PZ

Help those affected by 'winter blues or Seasonal Affected Disorder.

Lightboxes

Purchase from Larger Branches of Boots or direct from www.sadbox.co.uk.

SAMARITANS
Tel: 0845 790 9090

Confidential helpline with trained counsellors to help you find the way through difficult situations.

TRUE FREEDOM TRUST
P.O. Box 13
Upton
Prenton CH43 6YB
Tel: 0151 653 0773
www.truefreedomtrust.co.uk

Christian counselling/ support and teaching on homosexuality.

UNITED CHRISTIAN BROADCASTERS
PO Box 255
Stoke On Trent ST4 8YY
Tel: 0845 6040401
www.ucb.co.uk

Publish 'Word for Today' Produce Radio/TV programmes Satellite Channel 0125.

www.lookingforGod.com

UCB Prayerline
Tel: 0845 4567729

Prayer counselling available Monday to Saturday 9am to 10.30pm.

Wondering what to give to those who are "not yet Christians" who may be struggling with depression? Why not order our companion book

ESCAPE THE JUNGLE OF
DEPRESSION

Based on Christian Principles, but without scripture verses and, more importantly, without any jargon! Contains helpful advice and encouragement and some brief information about the Alpha Course. Great to buy for yourself or to pass on to a friend or relative who may be suffering with depression.

Price £7.50 + £2.50 p&p

Order any three for £20.00
(we will pay the postage and packing charges)

Orders to: Book requests New Day
15 Greave Close Rossendale Lancs BB4 8JT.

Please make cheques payable to New Day.